The Rose for Today

Growing the Beautiful Mini-Flora

By Sean McCann

*There are roses today that could never have
been envisaged 100 years ago; there are types
beyond human imagination; there are fragrances
to woo even the most unimaginative.
These are all dreams come true.*

American Rose Society

Published by:
American Rose Society
PO Box 30000
Shreveport, Louisiana 71130
Phone: 318-938-5402
http://www.ars.org

First Edition: July 2006

Printed in the United States

ISBN 0-9636340-6-2

On our cover: 'Madeline Spezzano', MinFl. Photo by Syl Arena.

Foreword
by American Rose Society President Marilyn Wellan

It is quite remarkable that, in our time, we rosarians are witnessing the emergence of an exciting new class of roses—the Mini-Flora. It is remarkable because it is rare that official new classes are added to the rose classification system. The last such addition to come along was grandiflora, which first appeared in *Modern Roses V* in 1958. In the preface of that edition, the arrival of the new class was reported with apparent hesitation and apprehension as to the longevity of the class.

The Mini-Flora—the "in-between" rose—thought by many to be a too-large miniature, only recently gained official recognition unto itself. Nurserymen who grew miniatures had been routinely discarding seedlings that were larger than the accepted standard for the class. Only after the larger blooms' imposing presence was recognized by keen exhibitors and growers as desirable, and only after those exhibitors and growers convinced others there really was a place for these gorgeous beauties, did the Mini-Flora gain support for the creation of a separate, official rose class. The American Rose Society, which has the responsibility for classification of roses, held numerous debates which were followed by much hand-wringing over the possible consequences, but finally the Mini-Flora was approved as a class of its own. Mini-Floras first appeared in our publications in the year 2000.

What happened after that was thrilling to witness. Larger new miniature roses were being registered as Mini-Floras in increasing numbers. Previously registered large miniatures were reclassified as Mini-Floras. Rose shows across the country eagerly added Mini-Floras to their show schedules. Excitement created by the emergence of the Mini-Flora also added to the success of the ARS National All-Miniature Rose Show, which included sections for the Mini-Flora beginning with its inaugural show in 1999.

Finally, we are all beginning to acknowledge what J. Benjamin Williams and Sean McCann have known for a long time—the gardening public would like to grow roses that fit their smaller gardens and busier lifestyles. Mini-Floras, often marketed as "patio roses," are ideal for growing in pots and in small spaces.

Now with widespread acceptance by serious rosarians and the rose-growing public, it appears what once was the undesirable, too-large miniature, the Mini-Flora, has found its place in the rose world. It appears the "in-between" bloom has overcome the long hesitation about its value, and—like grandifloras—they will be enjoyed in our gardens as long as roses are grown.

We are pleased that the American Rose Society has underwritten the publication of *The Rose for Today* through its Educational Endowment Trust. We are grateful to Mr. Williams and Mr. McCann for their lifelong contributions to the rose world, and especially for their heroic work in ensuring these treasured roses will be a part of the rose history we are witnessing today.

'Irene Watts', Hybrid China

'Dr. John Dickman', MiniFl

Introduction

by J. Benjamin Williams

Ben Williams is a hybridizer, horticultural consultant, nurseryman, and public relations leader for roses, and has been for many years. The new Mini-Flora rose is the result of his persistence and determination that the rose should be given its proper place in the gardens of the world.

Say hello to the Mini-Flora rose. It has been around nearly 30 years but has only recently been officially accepted as a separate class of rose. Its acceptance has given a new life to a beautiful new sort of rose: a plant that is easy to handle, lovely to look at, and as amenable and adaptable as any other rose that has gone before it.

The Mini-Flora began its existence when a few rose breeders found that by crossing miniatures with larger roses they produced an "in-between" plant, neither big nor small. Names were bandied about as to what they should be called—sweethearts, in-betweens, big minis or patios—but as far as officialdom was concerned, they were all to be regarded as miniatures or small floribundas. I began to find a large number of these lovely types in my breeding lines, and I determined to give them their proper place in the rose world. Success was slow in coming, so I trademarked the title Mini-Flora; but it still took many years to establish the designation within the rose community.

During the years, in my efforts to establish a place for this lovely rose, I had the help and encouragement of enthusiasts such as Bob Lindquist, Sam McGredy, Steve Hutton, Jacques Mouchotte, Henry Conklin, David Gilad, Alex Raab, Howard Walters, Ernest Schwartz, Robert B. Martin, Jr., members of the ARS classification committee and many others. The world-famous miniature breeder Ralph Moore was a great help too, by producing my first introduction of this classification. The rose was 'Patio Patty' and was introduced by the Conard-Pyle Company (Star Roses) of West Grove, PA.

Today hundreds of new varieties of the Mini-Flora rose are available. What is important is that we should explore the many ways they can be used. They are ideally suited for the gardener with limited space, whether living in an apartment or a private home. They may be grown in the garden or in containers. Their petite size makes them useful in borders or as bedding plants, in hanging baskets, or planted in containers on patios and terraces, as well as in window boxes. Small pots of the roses may be used to brighten up the steps to an entrance or as an accent along paths or walks.

Sean McCann, who has written this appreciation of the Mini-Flora, was one of the first garden journalists to appreciate that they had an important place in rose history, as he so stated in the British gardening press when he announced their introduction as Mini-Flora having patio as part of their name. So it is appropriate that now he should be the first author to tell the world about them. This book should convince everyone that the Mini-Flora is a beautiful, healthy and colorful addition to any garden. Everyone will quickly recognize its form and fragrance and grant it its place in the wonderful world of The Rose.

'Patio Patty', MiniFl

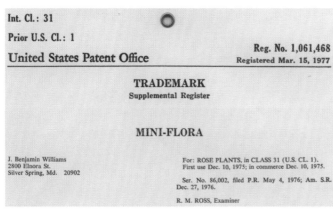

Int. Cl.: 31

Prior U.S. Cl.: 1

United States Patent Office

Reg. No. 1,061,468
Registered Mar. 15, 1977

TRADEMARK
Supplemental Register

MINI-FLORA

J. Benjamin Williams
2800 Elnora St.
Silver Spring, Md. 20902

For: ROSE PLANTS, in CLASS 31 (U.S. CL. 1).
First use Dec. 10, 1975; in commerce Dec. 10, 1975.

Ser. No. 86,002, filed P.R. May 4, 1976; Am. S.R. Dec. 27, 1976.

R. M. ROSS, Examiner

Mini-Flora Trademark Document

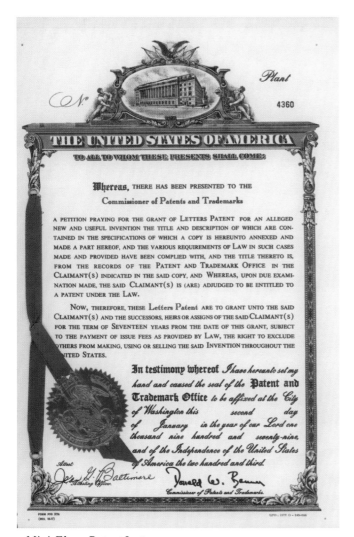

Mini-Flora Patent Letter

'Whirlaway', MinFl

Acknowledgments

No book can be written without the help of many people. I have been very lucky in my years of writing about roses to have found so many individuals who were always willing to help me with "awkward" questions. However I am always indecisive when it comes to giving acknowledgements that I make the greatest error of all – that of leaving someone out of the list. This has happened me before – and if it happens here again I hope for charity and forgiveness.

The roses named in this book belong to a new race of roses, aimed at today's living conditions. The people who encouraged me to write the book are many but certainly the initial impetus given was by J. Benjamin Williams, the man who brought these roses to the forefront. Without his input this book would not have been possible. His enthusiasm was infectious, his knowledge comprehensive, and his participation far-reaching. We met over a period of many years, always discussing this project.

His awareness was contagious and was backed by his family, plus the American Rose Society, through its former Executive Director, Mike Kromer, and the President of the Society, Marilyn Wellan. My deep appreciation must also go to the Educational Endowment Trustees of the American Rose Society for their belief in this book.

Among the many others who provided assistance on the way to publication are Phillip Schorr who provided an up-to-date record of Mini-Floras as of the date of publishing. Executive Director Michael Craft, Publications Director and Managing Editor, Beth Smiley and Educational Endowment Trustees.

The participation of rose breeders the world over was never withheld and many provided information and photographs for inclusion. Top photographers who have been generous in their participation are Rich Baer, P.A. Haring and Robbie Tucker. Within the family there has always been the greatest help – this time, Sally, my wife, our daughter, Oonagh, helped me read the script while "baby" son Ronan walked many a time through rose fields with me – putting up with my commentary on roses and life.

And where would a book be without an astute editor? Jeff Wyckoff was always helpful and kind and spotted many of my lapses and oversight in this book.

To them all my sincere thanks.

Sean McCann

'Topkapi Palace', MinFl

Contents

'Glamour Girl', MinFl

'Butter Cream', MinFl

Chapter 1
What Is the Mini-Flora Rose?

Roses are as diverse as anything nature has given us. From the hollowed out navel of a quartered rose to the bejeweled beauty of the almost single—the loveliness is there in roses a thousand years old and in roses as new as the dew of the morning.

Fashions will change, fads will pass, but beauty is eternal. A new world is born with every rose. And let us never forget that once upon a time every rose was new... and probably disliked by some just because it was new.

The Mini-Flora rose is something more than just another rose. If, for instance, you have ever wanted a rose garden but never had the space, along comes the Mini-Flora rose to add joy and beauty to your life.

To re-invent an old phrase, "cometh the hour, cometh the rose." Just when gardens around the world were becoming smaller and smaller and high-rise apartments and town houses were taking away the benefits of a space to grow beautiful roses, along came the rose for the occasion. It was big enough to be appreciated, small enough for the tiniest place and lovely enough for any enthusiast.

The Mini-Flora is a rose for everyone. It is the rose that has catapulted us into the 21st century.

Truth to tell, the world had been crying out for a rose like this for many years; a rose not as small as a miniature nor as big and bulky as many floribundas. A rose that can be grown anywhere; where, if you didn't have room for a small garden, it would happily perform in a container on a patio, veranda or balcony, and would grow cheerfully for years, seldom asking for much attention. In return for the little attention it needs, it will give the benefits of a beautiful rose for a long, long part of the year. A rose constantly attractive and reliable, with bushes producing colors ever varying, making every new bloom an adventure.

Like most good ideas the Mini-Flora took a little time to catch on. There were those dissidents who couldn't see a place or a need for it; after all, there were miniatures of every shape and color; there were floribundas of great distinction, so who wanted anything else.

'Tom Thumb', Min

'Wanaka', Min

However, anyone agreeing with that should be reminded of the continual pioneering spirit of the rose breeder. They are the fashion designers of the rose world, whose ideas are always developing, leading us into new situations with better plants, different concepts of fragrances, colors and plant shapes and sizes. Theirs is a constant search for significant advances to make the life of the gardener easier and more effective. They gave us the Mini-Flora.

Call it the adaptable rose. It is robust and easy to grow, with a variety of flower forms that range from the perfection of an abundant one-to-the stem small hybrid tea bloom to the mass profusion of a floribunda. In growth it should be about 18- to 24-inches high (although in some climates they will naturally grow bigger) and produce a mass of flowers over a long period. Overall the Mini-Flora gives the bonus of larger, more significant flowers and foliage than the miniatures and spreads over a much wider area. Grown in the ground or in containers, they have a high degree of winter hardiness as well as being very adaptable near the sea where salt sprays can often cause untold damage to many types of roses.

They are roses that need less attention, are less expensive to propagate, are more generous with their flowers and look good over a long period. In the past 10 years the beauty and adaptability of the Mini-Flora has reached a stage where now it has a very wide acceptability. Whether it is called Mini-Flora as in the United States or a patio rose as in Europe, it has shown just how effective it is. Today dozens of new varieties are there for the choosing with rose growers from every country adding to an ever-increasing range of varieties.

In modern rose terms it all began with the miniatures. At first they were small. Varieties like 'Tom Thumb' came out of Europe through the work of Jan de Vink in 1935; later from Spain's Pedro Dot came a string of successes such as 'Pour Toi'. The miniatures were then expanded in great variety and numbers by California's Ralph Moore, the wonder-man of miniature breeding, who produced little plants of infinite beauty. However, as time went on and the effect of the hybridizing methods increased, so too did the size of the roses. One researcher, the late Frank Buckley in the United Kingdom, recorded that even within a limited period of a few years in the second half of the 20th century, the average size of miniature rose plants increased in height by almost 12-inches.

So it was inevitable that the Mini-Flora would come along. Even before it received its international recognition people were talking about it and saw the possibilities of it adding new beauty to a garden.

What caught the attention is that they are compact, dwarf plants always covered with well-formed blooms, or as one producer calls them "flowers with a real rosebud and scent." They are great in the sun, happy in the rain, and in winter can withstand colder temperatures better, whether they are planted outdoors or grown in containers.

Their disease resistance became a byword too. They are healthier than many types that have gone before, a trait no doubt developed through the miniature rose parentage. Ralph Moore's edict was that rose breeding is like engineering: "You have to see things in their entirety before you set out with your plans. You have to dream for your special rose and then know how to engineer your way to it whether it takes two years or 20."

That is what J. Benjamin Williams did; after 30 years he achieved his perfect new rose. And with the assistance of the same Moore got the first plants of his new type of rose propagated.

What gardeners liked was the ease of maintaining these new roses. All the plant asked for was a good sunny spot in a rich, well-drained place, frequent enough watering to keep the soil moist, monthly fertilizing and some spraying to keep away insects and disease. Life for a rose is provided by sun, air, food and water—and then a little bit of love.

'Cuddles', Min

'Miss Alice', S

'Sparrieshoop', S

Chapter 2
How Did It Get Its Name?

One great rose man, Edward LeGrice, said that to appreciate roses you must have the skill of a craftsman, the vision of an artist, the persistence of a lover, and the trained eye of constant observation.

The interbreeding between small and big roses produced bushy, free-flowering smaller roses that in themselves meant little more than a headache for the breeder. They were neither floribunda nor hybrid tea. No one knew where they should be placed in the hierarchy of roses. For years there just was no acceptance for many lovely and useful varieties. Even as late as the 1970s few people saw the possibilities that these roses presented to the gardener. Indeed, in many a rose breeding house, seedlings that didn't fit into an existing classification were just culled and dumped.

That is why for so long the Mini-Flora rose was overlooked. You could ask for a miniature, a floribunda, a hybrid tea or any other sort of rose, but no one could ask for a Mini-Flora because it just didn't exist as a group. Whichever roses managed to get themselves through the net as regards to their size were just lumped together as small floribundas or big miniatures. And who wanted a big miniature? If you asked for a miniature you expected something small and dainty. If you requested a floribunda it had to be something that at least measured up to a normal waist height. The beautiful in-between roses were swamped.

World renowned rose breeder Sam McGredy described the situation when he said: "The original interest in patio/Mini-Floras came about because many breeders started to use Ralph Moore's miniature breeding exploits with their own. The resultant half-breed seedlings were neither one thing nor t'other. So, a new name had to be found."

As a writer on roses, I kept asking that something be done about giving a proper place in the rose world for these nomads. An answer was not so far away.

In his Maryland nursery, J. Benjamin "Ben" Williams was breeding roses; when he saw some of these larger miniatures coming through he asked himself the leading question: Why

'Patio Patty', MinFl

'Puppy Love', Min

'Classic Sunblaze', Min

should roses only be grown for those who have conventional gardens? It is the old business of asking the right question to get the right answer. And he had the right answer under his very nose. It was 1975 when he introduced a new rose called 'Patio Patty'. He had been looking at the rose for some time, always sure in his own mind that if people got to see it, they would love it. It was a low growing eye-catcher with great potential for those who could grow it on a terrace, balcony—or patio. It was too good not to let the public see it, but how could it be marketed if there was no acceptable classification?

Then the answer came to him—the rose was a cross between a floribunda and a miniature, so why not call it a Mini-Flora? But again, no one would listen to him. The classification authorities turned down his suggestion, with the result that the name Mini-Flora never got an airing. There was only one way left to go—to take a trademark on the classification name for himself.

He certainly never pretended that he was the first breeder ever to produce the dwarf-growing "Mini-Flora/patio" type rose, but he was one of the first to recognize its value and commercially extend its possibilities. The name fitted the new type of rose more than anyone initially appreciated.

"While everyone else was throwing away big minis, we were thinking of a more extensive breeding program to develop bigger and better ones and ways to promote and market them," he says. He asked Benny Hutton, former president of the Conard-Pyle Company, for his advice about his new in-between rose.

The mounded growth of the new rose, and especially its waxy foliage and cover of small multicolored blooms which went from ivory to yellow and peachy pink, impressed Hutton. After considering the row of 25 plants he gave his opinion: "It may be too big to be called a miniature and too small to be called a floribunda but that doesn't mean there is not a place in the rose world for it." So 'Patio Patty' became a reality and soon other breeders began to see the possibilities for their in-between roses. Many others also saw the great potential of the Mini-Flora group name. One of the first was the Meilland company in France. They had a group of roses they called "Sunblaze" that fit perfectly into the Williams category and they were quick to grasp the marketing opportunity. They introduced their Sunblaze roses in the Mini-Flora group with the permission of Ben Williams.

The Meilland roses were sold along with the Williams varieties for a number of years until the House of Meilland decided to trademark their big minis as Sunblaze roses, although many companies continued to market both the Meilland and the Williams varieties as Sunblaze and Mini-Flora roses. "There is no question that the Sunblaze roses, which are presently classified as miniatures in most places, could fall within the Mini-Flora class and have been sold in the USA by the Conard-Pyle Company (Star Roses) by the thousands for landscape and container purposes," says Williams, who believes current Meilland hybridizer Jacques Mouchotte was instrumental in producing many new Mini-Floras.

In other parts of the world roses of the same caliber were being sold as larger-than-minis-smaller-than-floribundas. One top American amateur breeder, Ernest Schwarz from Maryland, produced a great collection of roses including 'Cuddles', 'Puppy Love', 'Zinger', 'Sea Foam' and 'Pacesetter', some of which today could easily be classified as Mini-Floras. Among the professionals, Sam McGredy had developed a line using the Ralph Moore miniatures; other famous rose breeders such as Kordes in Germany, Harm Saville, Dee Bennett and Ernest Williams in the United States and Guys de Ruiter in Holland all saw this new type of rose developing among their seedlings. At first they called

'Zinger', Min

them in-between roses; then Pat Dickson of Northern Ireland, one of the world's top breeders, picked up on the name "patio roses" and that became the Mini-Flora group in Europe. He discussed the possibility of using the name with the late and famous breeder Jack Harkness, who wasn't too sure it had possibilities. But the Dickson nursery began offering them as multi-purpose roses, capable of being used anywhere in the garden. However, the roses did not receive general approval; after all, if a rose is called a patio rose, it seems to suggest it can only be grown there and, it was argued, these roses were just as effective in the garden. To justify the name, it was suggested that the patio "is a place where no one would think of growing a rose unless continually encouraged to do so." Hence, the continuance of the group name; and the emergence all over Europe of roses of this size under the collective name of patio.

'Sea Foam', S

Many others now followed the thought pattern of bigger-than-mini roses. Among these were the Poulsen empire of Denmark,

'Pacesetter', Min

'Bonbon Hit', MiniFl

'Regensberg', Fl

'Kaikoura', Min

where a magnificent range of roses have been developed. Many of these roses are definitely within the Mini-Flora standard. Their grouping is called the "Hit" series—'Bonbon Hit', 'Pink Hit', etc. Other Poulsen varieties include their tudor patios, which are listed under the group name "Palace" and are a floribunda type with lower growth and denser plants than the normal floribunda. In recent times Poulsens were having such a success with these that every second two of their roses were being sold somewhere in the 50 countries where these plants were marketed. These plants are all grown on their own roots and generally offered in a small pot with four rooted cuttings in flower.

Some striking plants in this size were developed by Sam McGredy. One of his best is still 'Regensberg', a beautiful hand-painted variety. It was produced in 1980 and is still considered a superb plant, but as he has commented with regret, it never quite made the top list. "That's a pity," he wrote in his book *Favourite Roses*, "because if I was going to end up on a desert island with just a few roses, 'Regensberg' is one I would bring with me." Although it is registered as a floribunda it is perfectly in the style of the Mini-Flora as seen by Ben Williams, and would certainly find a top place among the Mini-Floras. It is low, compact, hardy, healthy and always colorful with its lovely open blooms of cerise touched through with silver and with a silver reverse. Sam McGredy gave his opinion that "just about all of my so-called minis were too tall to be called miniatures. I guess 'Hauraki' (Rose of the Year, Auckland 1998), 'Manapouri', 'Kaikoura' and 'Wanaka' (also known as Longleat) were the best recognized as being possibles for the new classification."

Ben Williams feels that the term "patio" does not represent a good image or description of these roses. "A large majority of those so-called patio roses do not fall in the Mini-Flora class; many are too large and would more properly fall in another category as shrubs, ground covers or landscape roses. The aim should be to identify a proper classification for those roses which have been, and will be, developed in the future and marketed under their appropriate classification."

However there is the opposite argument that both climatic conditions and the propagation methods used have a great deal to do with the eventual size and possibilities of the roses. For instance, in many European countries (especially the United

Kingdom) the varieties are budded on to wild scions and this produces a much more vigorous bush. This makes it virtually impossible for all the European patio roses to fit under the umbrella of Mini-Floras. It is when patio roses are produced on their own roots that they begin to fit more and more into the whole concept of the Mini-Flora class. Until this has been accomplished many of the top patio roses will have to exist in their own limbo.

Elsa Spek of Jan Spek Rosen in Holland answered my query about the general attitude toward patio roses in their area. She said most garden people prefer the patio roses, which she describes as "bushy plants grown from cuttings in pots like all the fairy types and, in our case, varieties like 'Kent', 'Riverdance' and 'Peter Pan'. What really matters in these roses is the health of the plant." These varieties certainly live up to that standard.

'Kent', S

In Germany the top selling rose in this classification for the famous breeders Tantau are 'Golden Jewel' and 'Sugar Baby'. These are sold under the collective name of "Hobbit Roses" in 2- to 3-liter pots and are attracting a great deal of attention. Here again there is a great emphasis on disease resistance.

Outside Europe and the United States there tends to be a dilemma about these new small roses. For instance, in New Zealand many growers have placed various miniatures into the Mini-Flora grouping because they tend to grow tall, without any consultation with the breeders.

'Riverdance', Min

Sue O'Brien was among those who disagreed with the New Zealanders' decisions. Her mother Dee Bennett bred many of the world's most distinguished miniatures, and O'Brien felt that she should have been consulted before any of her mother's roses were arbitrarily sold as another type.

But New Zealand does have its own collection of valuable Mini-Flora roses. Frank Schuurman calls his the "fairytale" roses. These began with 'Tinkerbell', originally bred from 'Evelien', Peter llsink's spray rose, and 'White Dream' from Louis Lens. Over a period of 12 years these produced a series of plants in all colors and all with fairytale names. A few of his successes included 'Scentasia' (crème-yellow), Auckland Patio Rose of the year 1998 and Adelaide top patio of 1999; 'Thumbelina' (crème), Bronze award in Gifu, Japan 2000 and 'Peter Pan' (magenta-red) Silver Honor Medal in Rome 2001. Others in the series include 'Pinocchio' (purple), 'Snow White' (white), 'Aladdin' (coral),

'Golden Jewel', MinFl

'Snow White', Pol

'Merlot', Min

'Playmate', S

'Anastasia' (white), 'Apricot Scentasia', 'Goldilocks' (yellow) and 'Cinderella' (mauve).

Commenting about sales in his country, Schuurman notes: "All these are sold as garden patio roses, growing up to one meter tall with flowers from 3-5 cm in diameter, propagated on their own roots and grown on in 1.5- to 3-liter pots, taking about six to 12 months to be saleable."

In South Africa the name patio roses does nothing for Ludwig Taschner, one of the leading growers there. He says: "I shied away from using the patio rose group name mainly because patios in South Africa are areas covered with at least a heavy shading cloth material or a roof, and that is why we would rather use the expression "sunspot roses." With the present urge in using trademarked group names, we shall play with this much more in the future."

Taschner does acknowledge that great care must be taken when making a selection for this group, and that they must fall within the specific parameters of size in both bush and bloom that he has set out. "We are working on putting a group of varieties together which we will market in 12-inch pots under this brand. The criteria are blackspot resistance, pickable stems of about 9-inches long with hybrid tea shaped blooms of at least the size of a Mini-Flora (1.5-inches high, 2-inches wide for the open bloom) and a very free flowering growth habit. 'Playmate' from the late Colin Horner, 'Merlot' from Frank Benardella and 'Autumn Splendor' from Michael Williams are candidates.

"Another reason for the change in designation was that in our climate almost all the European patio roses have turned into very vigorous brutes with few flowers. Fryer's 'Sweet Dream' will easily grow to 10-feet high in one season with a few flowers on the tips of these long canes. The same applies to almost all of the Dickson patios.

"I also find it very difficult to differentiate between miniatures and Mini-Floras. Too many of the classical miniatures such as 'Magic Carrousel', 'Rise 'n' Shine', 'Ocarina' and 'Minnie Pearl' grow into hip-high little shrubs or hedges when not heavily pruned, and they carry flowers larger than on the short-pruned plants."

So around the world there are varying attitudes regarding the in-between roses. However, the big break in helping to distinguish between the various types has now evolved, mainly through the persistence of Ben Williams. The credit and the eventual acknowledgement of Mini-Flora roses is totally due to his influence. He has pushed for their recognition since the 1970s, when he registered the trademark of Mini-Flora. But authorities are slow to respond. Williams never gave up pushing for an international general classification from the American Rose Society for the mounting group of roses which have been left in an indeterminate state. Eventually the coin dropped, as both rose growers and breeders saw the expanding possibility for these roses once they could be classified. They were willing to talk—and no one was more prepared to do this than Ben Williams. He again offered the rights to the trademark "Mini-Flora" to the American Rose Society, free of charge. This time they accepted, and so a legitimate place was found for the lost roses.

This recognition is very important. "Whether it is called a patio rose or a Mini-Flora doesn't really matter," says Williams, " the fact is that, with its recognition within the rose world, it has rescued a whole batch of very fine and acceptable roses from extinction."

Today these fabulous new roses add to the beauty and charm of gardens and give those who are not able to garden the chance to have the same beauty in a simple or elaborate container. They bloom almost from spring to winter and give masses of flowers as fragrant as your nose will admit and as robust as any before them. And to widen the scope of the class, there are also opportunities for their exhibition in rose shows. These roses-in-limbo have found their place in the whole spectrum of gardens and show benches. When you talk of wonders in the garden, the Mini-Flora rose is a true wonder.

'Cinderella', S

'Autumn Splendor', MiniFl

'Aladdin', Min

'Miss Alice', S

Chapter 3
Old-Fashioned Patio Types

Where would we be if humanity had never known the rose? If roses didn't exist or had been hidden from view...our character, our morals, our aptitude for beauty, for happiness—would they be the same?

There were smaller growing, bushy roses long before the modern varieties arrived. For instance, among old garden roses there are many varieties that could well fit into the same garden and growing settings as the Mini-Flora.

Call them Mini-Floras of the past (most of them will be found under the classification of polyantha roses) and you can go back over a century and find references to many of them.

In the mid-1800s William Paul, hybridizer, grower and author, wrote that diminutive roses were often planted in masses "in which manner they look well, as they are of neat growth, and bloom profusely...the china and bourbon roses are usually preferred for dwarf masses, and no wonder, when it is considered that they produce their beautiful flowers during one half of a year."

He was one of the early believers that roses in containers did very well. "It is no longer said the rose is intractable as a pot plant; indeed it is now sufficiently established that it is perfectly suited for that purpose." And to prove the point he wrote in many of his famous rose books in the early 1800s on this very subject, giving many pages and illustrations to it in his famous publication, *The Rose Garden.* Not having them in pots, he argued, would leave a great blank in the rose grower's world. How that would apply today!

As early as 1848 there were rose varieties, many of which are considered miniatures today, that earned their reputations by their perpetual flowering, as well as by being dwarf and robust. One of the earliest was 'Pompon de Paris' (a small china rose, medium-pink, 1839). While you can find this rose in catalogs today, the majority of those bred in this same era sadly slipped away. But they didn't stay hidden, and in the 1920s made a comeback that resulted in an explosion of smaller roses.

Suddenly rose growers found themselves with a backlog of low-growing roses that could easily fit into the now emerging

'Perle d'Or', Pol

'Marie Pavié' , Pol

'Yvonne Rabier', Pol

container-type category, bringing with them a touch of old world charm. Among a number that were identified by the growers were 'Little White Pet' (1879), 'Perle d'Or' (golden yellow, 1884), 'Marie Pavié' (white with flesh centers, 1888), 'Yvonne Rabier' (pure white, 1910), 'Pride of Hurst' (coral-pink, 1926), 'Cameo' (salmon-pink, 1932), 'The Fairy' (light pink, 1932), 'Doris Ryker' (salmon-pink, 1942) and 'China Doll' (rose-pink, 1946), all of which are now classified as polyanthas. Into much the same category came the lovely 'Mlle Cécile Brünner' (1881), which became known as the "Sweetheart Rose" because of its exquisitely shaped tiny pink blooms.

Other famous names from the past now beginning to emerge in catalogs include the apricot-pink 'Irene Watts' (a china rose, 1896) and the deep burgundy-red 'Louis XIV' (hybrid perpetual, 1859). But while these are small plants (in most places) they do not have the abundant foliage that is generally accepted in the modern Mini-Flora.

While I am not suggesting for one moment that these varieties should be considered in the modern Mini-Flora classification, it is always worth considering using them in much the same way. They all take happily to container growing, and with their softly fragrant, informal blooms, are true eye-catchers. For a touch of the past, any of these lovely varieties, with their old-fashioned growth and foliage, will fit in with a planting of today's Mini-Floras, which, to quote (out of context) the words of William Paul, "such a combination of desirable properties must necessarily secure for it a large share of favour."

English Roses

English hybridizer, grower and author David Austin made a huge breakthrough a quarter century ago with a group of roses that he called "English Roses." He married the charm of the old roses with that of the modern roses and produced varieties that carry cupped, quartered and rosette type blooms. They have become one of the top sellers of the past 25 years. Initially his productions were tall, leggy and hardly compatible with a book on low-growing roses for the garden.

Eventually, lower-growing varieties did emerge, and today there are a number of low-growing types that can fill the same setting as required for the Mini-Floras, although even his lowest growing varieties tend to grow taller than the accepted Mini-Flora size (size can change according to climate conditions). However, they do provide an old-fashioned look with their distinctive flower shapes, and also carry a desirable fragrance into the bargain.

One of my own favorites is 'Glamis Castle', a white, robust and low-growing variety that looks good when placed just out of immediate range and providing backup for the Mini-Floras. However, this one has often been said to be blackspot susceptible, although I have grown numerous bushes of it over the years and it has never been much worse than many other roses. Others considered by many to be small enough to fit into the category include the apricot 'Ambridge Rose', the buff-colored 'Bredon', deep magenta crimson 'Noble Antony' and deep rose-pink 'The Mayflower', all of which can be kept very happily short. As well as these, the 2001 introduction 'Miss Alice' fits into the Mini-Flora ideal, being very compact, free flowering and healthy. So the future of the Mini-Flora could also see some of the English Roses included in their number.

'Glamis Castle', S

'The Mayflower', S

'Pompon de Paris', Ch

'Sweet Dream', Fl

Chapter 4

Planting

You can always dig a better hole. It might sound like the title of an old Music Hall song, but in fact it is the best advice that someone about to plant roses could ever get.

Today, because of increasing interest, you can purchase the Mini-Flora in two different ways—either as an own-root or as a budded plant. "Own-root" means that the plants have been grown from cuttings and will have a dense root system with more fibrous roots. This makes them more easily grown in containers where the roots will be able to fetch moisture and fertilizer from a restricted growing area. Budded roses have stronger, longer roots with very little fibrous growth, which means they need a deeper area for planting. These are often the better sort for outside growing, where the tap root system can search deeper for its nutrition.

Just making a slit in the ground and hoping that nature will take over and nurture your rose is wishful thinking. Planting outside means giving the rose a proper home. Even when they are used in conjunction with other roses, the gardener must remember that Mini-Floras should have a frontal position because of their size. Planting them behind other roses means they will not get the necessary light or nutrition to prosper.

In beds on their own, either at ground level or as raised beds, as borders or as small hedges, they can be spectacular. As a carpet of roses they are exceptional—usually a great deal better than the effect provided by ground cover varieties.

In fact, you hardly need to search for somewhere to plant them. They can be grown everywhere and by everyone. They are the easiest of all plants to place in a garden, a patio or a veranda. They are happy in a container, or in the ground. Just give them a vital sun spot where they can also be supplied with water, food and a little bit of love and you will find they are the easiest of all roses to grow. If you yearn for a rose garden in a confined space, there is nothing more interesting than a group of containers with these roses on a patio, or outside a front door as a welcoming gesture.

They have established themselves as great varieties for giving

'Mlle Cécile Brunner', Pol

'China Doll', Pol

'Bredon', S

flowers all spring and summer, and often deep into autumn. Get into the habit of always having another plant coming along, and you will find that when one is tired and needing a little rest (think of it as a siesta), there is another one ready to take its place. That way you need never be without a blooming rose around your house and garden.

Their uses in containers are virtually inexhaustible. There are low-growing varieties that will spread over the edges of containers or window boxes, troughs or barrels, and there are taller varieties that just present themselves as a mass of blooms where the container is the least admired thing about the planting.

If expense doesn't matter, there is a huge variety of containers that will do justice to your new plants. While those magnificent urns or large glazed pots are wonderful to look at, they are not that practical for those who may want to move them around the garden—unless there is a potential weightlifter in the family. This also applies to the placing of half whiskey barrels, which are also very heavy to move. Reflect too on their placing before putting them somewhere where you may want to move them fairly frequently. The way to use these heavy containers is to place a smaller and lighter container inside them. These can then be changed or moved when the plant is taking a rest.

However, these roses are the least demanding of all types and they can be grown in just about any container that is handy; if that particular container is not up to your decorating requirements, then the roses themselves will soon cover the deficiencies, as their foliage can fall down and cover any ugliness that might be there.

Just make sure the style of container you use has good drainage. Frequently large ceramic pots do not contain drainage holes and can create a disaster that cannot be rectified. Some types of containers—notably terracotta pots—seem to need much more frequent watering because they perspire. Roses planted in containers of any sort also need regular feeding, despite the fact that the majority of potting composts have enough fertilizer for an extended period of about three months. My own belief is that a little soluble fertilizer every other week when watering keeps the plants happy. Slow-release fertilizer pellets can be used instead. However, once the watering-plus-soluble-sustenance technique has been established, the plants seem to be much happier.

Every two years container-grown plants will need a little extra attention. This is the time to change some of the compost and possibly prune back any roots that seem to be looking for room to grow. Check out the roots; if they are limp, brown and lack luster, something needs to be done. Roots should be white, energetic and thriving. Give the plant a good pick-me-up tonic. Start with a good soaking and later add a small amount of soluble fertilizer. If the roots are growing through the bottom of the container, it is time to lift the plant out and add some new compost at the base, or change the container size. Do not wait too long if your plant looks unhealthy; that is usually a warning that there are some pests that have formed their own colony there and are eating the roots. *(Check the Trouble Shooters Guide, Chapter 10)*

If the plant looks healthy and is growing the way you want it to, then just rake away some of the top soil—about an inch or two—and renew it with well-enriched potting compost.

Any problems that may arise will be easily spotted if you have been giving your plant that little piece of vital encouragement that goes along with the watering, feeding, sun, good air circulation and a little extra TLC. Much the same goes for hanging baskets. These, more than any other type of container, need repeated watering and regular feeding as well as a sunny spot. Instead of planting directly into the hanging basket, put the Mini-Flora plant into a suitable pot and then place this in the hanging basket, filling in around the vacant part with some sphagnum moss, which will also help conserve moisture. These pots can then be removed when the plant needs a thorough soaking, a process that is not always easy with a hanging basket. Putting some soil polymers, water crystals or polymer crystals in the soil is the answer to water shortage. This is a white granular material that absorbs hundreds of times its weight in water and can last for years, so even if you forget to keep the plant watered, your forgetfulness won't be fatal to the rose.

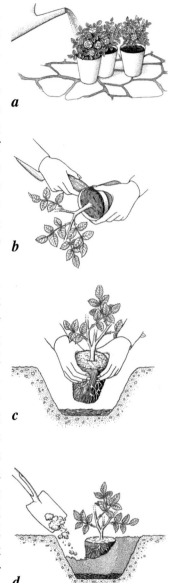

a

b

c

d

Planting out potted miniatures is simple enough, provided the area has been thoroughly prepared. Water the pots and then gently tip the rose out keeping the root wall together.

'Sweet Arlene', MinFl

Chapter 5

Indoor Growing

It used to be said that God gave us memories so we could have roses in winter. Today we can have the real roses in winter, courtesy of the same God.

Do Mini-Floras grow well indoors? Well, they do—and they don't. In my experience they will last quite happily for a number of weeks in normal household conditions, provided they are well looked after. But not everyone agrees. From New Zealand I got an opposite view from Frank Schuurman, a man who has built a very successful business both breeding and growing roses for indoor use. Speaking about the small pot-grown supermarket plants, he believes they are definitely not indoor plants and will go down hill very quickly and "disappoint the customer in the process."

However, many people (myself included) have had success with this sort of plant in a normal household situation, especially when there are no roses available from the garden. If you decide to bring your Mini-Flora indoors, the main requirement is to use small own-root plants that should be given light, water, air and good loose soil. Hot sun or no sun are problems, but somewhere in between is ideal. Find them a nice sunny place between 65 and 70 degrees; they will not do well in a dry atmosphere and will enjoy being sprayed occasionally with a fine mist of water on the foliage. They must be kept moist at all stages, so discipline yourself to look after them on a daily basis. A weak fertilizer added to the watering, which should be good and regular, will provide as close to an ideal micro-climate as can be achieved in open house conditions. Provide adequate drainage facilities. When they have finished flowering or look droopy and listless, that is the time to put them in the open again, where a shady warm spot will quickly revive them, after which they can be brought indoors. Many plants fail because central heating or air conditioning has dried them up.

But having said this, I should emphasize that successful indoor growing of Mini-Floras (or any other roses, for that matter) should be carried out in a manner where conditions have been specially created. Suggested essentials include two 40-watt light bulbs at either end of the table or bench where you want to grow your plants and a small fan nearby to keep the air moving; these will keep the plants moist. A capillary mat underneath them is also very useful. Nourish them regularly with a weak solution of a soluble fertilizer in water.

However, the person who purchases one or two plants to decorate the house will find it a different experience. Roses are plants for the garden or the greenhouse, and it will have to be an exceptional plant (with a very good minder) that will survive the rigors of indoor pot growing for longer than a few weeks.

Here is the Easy Care Way:
• Never let your pot plants dry out. If they are left without water for a long period of time they will suffer with bud drop and loss of foliage.
• Sharpen your intuition; look at your roses constantly and you will soon learn when they need watering. Give them enough but never too much.
• Water directly into the pot, never over the plant itself.
•Make sure they are given sufficient nutrition. Add a liquid fertilizer every time they need watering. This applies especially when they are forming new growth and flower buds. A little applied often is always the best way to feed. Follow the instructions on the package of the soluble fertilizer.
•When they are in flower they need much less nutrition.
•At the arrival of autumn stop adding fertilizer to the water. This is when the plant needs a little time to help build up its strength for the winter.
•Keep the plants flowering by cutting off dying blooms; just nip the little flower under the head and the plant will soon produce new blooms.

'Pink Hit', Min

'Tennessee Sunrise', MinFl

Chapter 6

In The Garden

To meet my roses without some ignorance is to lose a tiny sense of adventure. The parallel to a love affair is obvious.

In the open garden Mini-Floras may be used in front of bigger roses (plant them on the sunny side where they are not shaded by taller plants). While it is true that they are more versatile in smaller gardens than in larger ones, they do have their own special qualities. As edging they do spectacularly well, especially in a border or bed where the larger roses have become leggy, as many do when they have not been pruned correctly or grown well. The smaller plants quickly conceal leggy, woody growth and provide a welcome mat of color at their feet. Provided the soil is in good condition—the best soil is a good medium loam that does not get too heavy and never gets waterlogged—they will be very generous and rewarding in flowering.

Versatility is the real word that should go with these roses. Most of them provide bushy plants that will give a massed effect when placed about 12 to 18 inches apart. Just give the rose room to establish itself and then let it get on with its own life.

The planting spot is the powerhouse for the future of your rose, and the better you make it, the better your rose will grow. Take this as your slogan: it is not so much the roses in your life as the life in your roses that counts. But before you begin planting, you had better get the planning right. To put it another way, if you plant a rose in the right spot, there is nothing like it; if you plant a rose in the wrong spot, there is nothing like it either!

Right and wrong spots begin when you look at your garden and make the decision on how and where you are going to grow your Mini-Floras. Roses, you will be told, will grow just about anywhere, and so they will. They will survive wind, rain, sun, dry heat, high humidity and cold fog without complaint. But the quality of growth will vary so much that the gardener who puts even a little time and effort into planning their future home will be repaid many times over.

I have one easy way of selecting a site for a new rose bed. Before I do anything else I ask myself one question: "Would I like to spend most of my time in this spot if I was a rose?" If the

'Elizabeth Munn', Min

answer is no, then I change things.

Like so many worthwhile plants, roses need an airy, well-drained, sunny place to give their best. Airy and sunny doesn't mean they have to be planted by themselves in the middle of a garden where the wind will whip them from every side and where the sun will burn their hearts out at the height of its power.

Airy simply means giving them space away from walls, hedges and fences so air can circulate around and through them. It means keeping them away from large trees, clumps of shrubs or hedges that will greedily take away all the nutrients and moisture from the soil and leave them close to the starvation point. These same hedges and trees may also deprive the roses of sun. Frequently plans are made for rose plantings after autumnal leaf fall and before summer growth, since a site may look quite light and airy in winter or early spring but in summer will be overhung with heavy foliage.

Sunny means morning sun, if possible, for about six hours. If they get that they will tolerate, and even enjoy, a little afternoon shade. Don't forget, however, that a rose that sits in constant sunshine will need a considerable amount of watering to keep it from wilting.

"Well drained" is often a phrase that bothers gardeners, and it is legitimate to ask why, if roses like water, they need to be well drained? The point is they do not like to stand all day with cold roots and hot heads, and standing in stagnant water does not help either. If water forms around the roots of a rose, the plant will struggle against it, and it will eventually die.

So how do you find out if the site drains adequately? Dig a trial hole to a depth of about 12 to 18 inches and fill it with water. If the water drains off within a few hours the site is fine. If it doesn't, and if the water is still there after 24 hours, then drainage will have to be provided, another site found or a raised bed made.

Drainage can be improved by digging off, but retaining for future use, the topsoil and adding a layer of gravel or volcanic cinder at the base. This will take care of most problems, but if the situation is more acute it will need a more definite approach. The most complete way to solve a drainage problem is to dig a trench beneath the planting site and, by using pipes, drain tiles, or hollow blocks, make a soakaway that will carry the water toward a drain, ditch or sewer. Before placing soil back over the drain, any openings in the pipe should be covered by tiles, roofing felt or plastic to prevent soil from washing in and clogging up all your good work. The point where the drain begins should also be covered tightly, as roots from hedges and trees will find their way to it and eventually clog it.

A popular way to build rose beds in very wet areas is to make a raised bed. Clear the area to be planted, then thoroughly mix some good light soil, organic matter and gritty sand in with the top layer of soil you have dug out. For additives you will need some manure (preferably from a stable where the horses have been bedded down in wood shavings, peat moss or alfalfa hay), about 20 pounds of alfalfa meal or pellets (for a 50-square-foot bed), 10 pounds of gypsum, and about 3 pounds of superphosphate (0-20-0), all well tilled in. There may be some alterations to this formula in local areas, so I suggest any potential rose growers should search out their local rose societies and take advice from a Consulting Rosarian of the American Rose Society, or your own national rose society. This is basically the mix that will really let your roses take off. The bed can then be constructed within a framework of wood, stone or metal. In cold areas it is useful to remember that wood products such as landscaping timbers or railroad ties will provide better insulation.

'Spring's A Comin'', MinFl

Once the site has been decided upon, the next step is to establish the growing qualities of the soil. The perfect pH for rose growing is from 6.5 to 6.8; in other words, a slightly acidic soil. To check your soil, you can purchase small kits that work reasonably well, or you can send a soil sample to one of the many laboratories in your locale or around the country. The results from these may vary from the fairly general to those (usually more expensive) that will give detailed reports as well as recommendations for any improvements needed. If they say you need something added to your soil, believe them! Most troubles will be avoided if you can build up some quality planting soil.

A few years ago I saw a large quantity of roses being planted in soil that, before it was worked, would probably have been good enough for most gardeners. However, the rosarians involved knew well the good basics that are needed in this situation and they went further. Wanting only the very best, they brought in a digger to make all the holes 2 feet x 2 feet. Then, mixing sawdust, year-old straw from a dairy, mushroom compost, *Osmocote*, bone meal

'The Fairy', Pol

'Golden Anniversary', MinFl

and cottonseed meal, they filled goody bags and, splitting them as they went along, left one in each hole! And that was only for starters; watering and regular fertilizing came later.

Maybe this is too much to ask of the ordinary gardener or rose lover, but if you can emulate that, go to it now! Whatever else you skimp on when planting a rosebush, don't be a miser about the soil. This is the factory for your roses for years to come. Any improvements you make will be well repaid. To make it simple, remember the old advice that a mixture of sincerity and horse manure makes for great rose growing conditions.

To add interest to any planting of Mini-Floras or patio roses, a standard or rose tree in the same color will add greatly to the whole scene by adding height. When planting a tree rose, a stake is necessary so that the stem does not get broken in winds. Make this stake from metal or treated wood so that it will not rot. Too often the stake is positioned above the rose head or, far worse, just halfway up the stem. Just below the large flower head is the correct place to tie the rose and stake together—preferably with a stretchable tie or, in the old fashioned way (and showing my age), with a strip of nylon stocking. These will prevent rubbing or damage to the bark.

Your Outdoor Planting Plans
•A sunny, well-drained site is the first essential.
•Raised beds make it much easier to see the full effects of the Mini-Flora.
•Life becomes so much easier when making beds for these roses. Any shape, pattern or design will suit their low-growing nature.
•Ensure there is a watering source nearby to make life easier for the water carrier.
•As a centerpiece in a bed, consider tree or standard roses to give height and draw the eye.
•Large beds can look awkward with smaller roses, so instead of making one big bed, consider planting a number of smaller beds within the large one. To make the most effective use of the Mini-Floras or patio varieties, plant them in groups of five. Single bushes never look quite as happy as those planted in groups.
•Avoid mixing different varieties within a bed. This circumvents the problem of one type growing taller or spreading more than the others. In terms of color, the influence of one-of-a-sort varieties

is far more eye-catching than something with the bewildering color effect of a bag of *Skittles*.

Pruning

Pruning was once an art. You searched for various details about the bush before you made a cut. Even Shakespeare made a stab at it when, in *Richard II*, he wrote:"Superfluous branches/ we lop away so that bearing boughs may live." Great advice, but like so much lore about pruning, not totally applicable when working with the Mini-Flora. As far as the accepted method of pruning goes, forget it. Life's too short for that (and so is this rose). All you need do is to take the garden shears to the bush and clip away until you have reached the height and shape you want. Every three or four years cut out the old wood that has bloomed itself out. This, in itself, will rejuvenate the bushes.

The Mini-Flora breaks freely from the base every year so there is enough growth on all bushes to allow them to be cut back to about half size in the early spring, with a topping back, if necessary, in the middle of August. During the blooming season pinch off the dead flowers and forget all the lore about going down to outward facing eyes and five leaflet groups. Call this the cut-and-come-again rose.

Remember these points and you will have a lifetime of beauty and satisfaction from your Mini-Flora roses.

'California Heart', MinFl

'What a Peach', S

Chapter 7

Propagating Techniques for the Gardener

Learn how to do it, and you will never be without a fresh rose plant in your life.

Rose breeders don't have simple ideas—they have dreams. Dreams of breeding wonderful roses, novel roses, fragrant roses, roses that will last forever. But you cannot live by dreams alone. When Sam McGredy, one of the most prolific and illustrious rose breeders of our time, wanted to see the day when all roses would be as easy to grow as geraniums, there were many skeptics about.

It was easy to scoff at this idea because, at that time in the 1970s, it seemed an unlikely event. Most roses were propagated generally by either budding, grafting or tissue culture. Today most of these methods have been left to the professionals. The method increasingly used today (except for the United Kingdom where this method has not caught on) is to grow the roses on their own roots.

The breakthrough came from miniature roses, which provided the plank on which the McGredy strategy was based. The small roses began to infiltrate the window boxes and hanging baskets of gardens everywhere. They were easy to grow and were proving their own popularity. It was only a short leap before growers began to look at the propagation of bigger roses by the same means as that employed with the little roses.

This method is to grow the roses on their own roots from simple pieces of cuttings taken from the mother plants. Today, this technique is used to also produce old garden roses, shrubs, floribundas and climbers. However, some hybrid teas have proved to be less than cooperative, and many are not easy to grow from cuttings. But the Mini-Floras have shown themselves to be as accommodating, generous and forgiving as any rose can be— probably because they have in their makeup the buoyant blood of the miniatures, and this is making them a great market mover when grown on their own roots.

Plants made from this method are usually quite small and need time to develop; however, mature they do, and most tend to be less liable to destruction from garden pests, family animals or simply the weather because the root system will continue to send

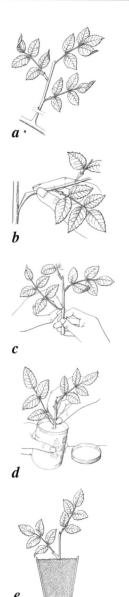

Mini-Floras grow very easily from cuttings. Select a cutting that has carried a flower and either cut it (a) or take a heel slip (b). Trim off the bottom two sets of leaves (c). Dip the cutting in a roosting powder or gel (d) and then simply plant in a small pot (e) with a good cutting compost.

up new shoots where other roses (budded or grafted) would be less inclined. It is often the case that where a budded or grafted rose is destroyed or badly injured, the root will only send up suckers from the wild stock used for its propagation. The own-root Mini-Flora will reproduce itself perfectly from a cutting.

When I stated earlier that it is a versatile rose, I should have added that its tolerance level has to be experienced to understand its acceptability.

Most Mini-Floras give a positive response to efforts to get them to root. There are many different ways to approach the rooting. Some gardeners may be in a position to have a misting house or box where cuttings can receive proper attention, thus avoiding the problems of humidity and rot. Not many of us have this luxury however, so different methods must be approached. These include taking a cutting and actually sticking it in the same pot as the parent plant, putting it in a small container by itself with a general compost, or taking three or four cuttings and placing them around the perimeter of a pot. I have seen them rooted in simple floral foam (the material used by flower arrangers), in large containers and even hanging from glasshouse beams in tiny pots. *Ziploc* bags have also been used advantageously—put a couple of inches of damp soil in the bag, insert the cuttings and finally close the bag tightly before hanging it up in a warm but semi-shady area. There are even some varieties that have been said to grow by simply throwing them at some soil to take off! Or as one old gardener said to me once: "You only have to spit at them to get them to root!"

Preparation

Old, hard wood is difficult to root, while young, tender growth will generally wilt before it roots. Select instead a cutting or stem that has just bloomed. First, remove the bloom. This should leave about 6 inches of wood with four sets of leaflets. Remove the bottom two sets and cut the stem just below the eye where the bottom leaflet was removed, leaving the top three sets of leaves on the cane.

Never allow cuttings to dry out. Put them into a small container of water or wrap them in a wet kitchen towel until planting time. Some gardeners leave the cuttings for a while in a vitamin B solution, but I have never found it any better than water. One tip

I *have* found that increased the rooting capabilities of the cutting is to damage the end with a fingernail or even a nail file. Scoring the cuttings with multiple tiny incisions on the base seems to encourage more roots to grow from the damaged areas.

These cuttings tend to root easily in small pots filled with a potting compost mixed with the same amount of perlite. Dip the bottom end of the cutting into a hormone rooting powder or liquid. Make a hole in the potting soil with a pencil and firm it up after the cutting is inserted. Cover with a plastic bottle, such as those used for sodas, with the bottom end removed and the cap left off. Again, this is a case of using your intuition. If the cuttings are to be left in a very sunny spot, an opaque bottle will be best; if they are grown in duller conditions, a clear bottle is ideal.

Of course this is just one way; I call it my dummies method. However, the Mini-Flora cuttings don't seem to mind how they are treated. As well as the above method, you can grow them in just about any type of container, even under the mother bush or sheltered by another rose to give them shade when it is needed.

In about four to five weeks, the cuttings should have rooted. I have often heard the advice given that to know when a cutting has rooted, you should give it a "tug" (hold yourself back), a gentle little suggestion of a pull that will let you know if some roots are holding the cutting in place. If it seems to resist the tug, just leave it alone and let it get on with its own style of growth.

Many gardeners worry about what they should do regarding feeding and care once the roots have formed. The perfect answer is given by Mary S. Pullen, who is regarded in the United Kingdom as one of the foremost amateurs in this respect. Whenever I have a rose of my own that is hard to root I mail a cutting to Mary, and her success rate is wonderful.

Her advice is: "I do not feed the cuttings whilst they are making root in the sterile cutting medium. The search for food improves root development. Once the cuttings have taken, I usually repot them into a mixture of any peat-based compost and perlite. I do not feed them for about two to three weeks, and then I usually start them off with a quarter-strength soluble fertilizer or any powdered food that will dissolve in water. I usually try to pot them as soon as the roots start to come through the bottoms of the pots, which if kept a little on the dry side, seems to speed the process: I find that when placed in fresh compost this will

f

g

h

i

Make sure that your cutting is kept moist (f) but not too wet. A small plastic bag tied over the cutting will provide a good home until the roots begin (g). When the plants have become established and the summer is approaching, they can be planted out (h) just like any other potted plant. Otherwise they can be left to grow on in pots for a number of years—all that is needed then is to change the pot size as the plants get older and bigger.

feed them for a while anyway. The amount of water and feed they need depends a lot on the weather and the conditions where they are grown. Sunny, bright, warm weather will obviously call for more watering than in duller, cooler conditions."

Propagation by means of cuttings is the way everyone is looking to succeed with their roses. It is simpler, the roses are better quality and although they may be smaller to begin with, they soon catch up.

As a final note on propagation, readers should be aware that it is illegal to asexually propagate—to start by budding, grafting or through cuttings—any rose variety that is under patent. United States patent laws protect a variety for 20 years from the date of issuance of the patent.

'Andie MacDowell', MinFl

'Seattle Sunrise', MiniFl

'Violet Mist', MinFl

Chapter 8

Showing

It is time to let them be what they really are — maxi-minis — and let the hybridizer bring them into their own court of honor in a rose show. – the late Bob Whitaker in The Rose Leaf, *bulletin of the Nashville Rose Society.*

If someone had asked me when my real enthusiasm for growing roses began, I would have to say it was the day I entered a rose show. That was many years ago — too long ago to date here!. I went along with some roses picked straight from the garden, a complete dummy to the whole business of showing roses. I knew nothing, so expected nothing. But I did win, and that was the immediate incentive I needed, so the next week I was at another show. And I won again!

Winning was nothing more than taking home a card marked "First Prize." The spur was the competition. It gave a new dimension to my rose growing. The people were different, the excitement was great and the winning was fun too! One memorable day I swept the board at a show; every first prize card and trophy fell to me. Then I was hooked.

I continued to show roses for a number of years, going to extraordinary lengths to take my roses around the world. The most distinctive method I found was on the ferryboat across the Irish Sea. When I wanted to get my roses from my home in Ireland to England in top condition, I took them to the ferry and put them into the mortuary which was always empty…and it was cool in there. Taking them to America needed a great deal of trust, since I had not discovered the wonderful boxes that people like Dr. Tommy Cairns and the late Lt. Col Maurice Gross used as they criss-crossed the Atlantic, keeping their roses in top condition.

Until very recent times there was no place for the Mini-Flora on the show bench. Some roses like 'Cachet', which is now classified as Mini-Flora, were registered as miniatures. In 1997 'Cachet' won Queen of the Show in the American Rose Society's Fall National Convention in Shreveport, LA. It was a stunning bloom, but caused quite a bit of controversy by being one of the biggest "miniature" blooms ever to be awarded this prize. Some years ago, while judging at a major Royal National Rose Society

'Camden', MinFl

'Bella Via', MinFl

show in England, I had no hesitation in awarding the best bloom in the section to a very large miniature—the coffee-colored 'Evita'. That met with a lot of discussion, too.

In those days before the Mini-Flora classification was confirmed, many beautiful blooms like these were denied the major awards by judges working in line with the *Guidelines for Judging Roses*; today the old language has been replaced by rules that state the bloom must be "typical of the variety."

Robbie Tucker, who has established himself as a hybridizer, exhibitor and lecturer, has met with the intolerance of some judges. "As an exhibitor and a judge, I saw much prejudice both for and against larger minis. The change the ARS has made to allow the Mini-Flora to be eligible for Queen is a good decision. In time, as hybridizers begin to fill this new class, I believe the Mini-Flora will eventually have its own Queen of Show. Right now, this may not seem like a good idea to many, but I believe it will be a natural transition in a few years."

Sue O'Brien, judge, grower and inheritor from her mother, the late Dee Bennett, of some of the world's best miniatures, admires the arrival of the Mini-Flora for showing. "With the advent of the Mini-Flora class, minis that previously were too large to be considered good exhibition varieties are being judged as 'great' Mini-Floras for show. This is proven by the number of Mini-Floras chosen for miniature Queen and other significant awards in shows."

So now the Mini-Flora is finding its way, and already rose shows all around America have specific classes for them. In the space of a very few years, entries of Mini-Flora roses at district and national level shows have gone from two to three to hundreds, and many societies are offering more and more classes and awards. Show chairs, judges and show committee and classification committee members are now including, as well as expecting, to expand the class in each show.

Encouragement for the participation of Mini-Floras in shows has been given by the founder of the class, Ben Williams, whose trophy, the J. Benjamin Williams Mini-Flora National Trophy, is offered at the two national rose shows in the United States. It was first awarded at the Atlanta Fall National Rose Show in 2000. The blooms that took the trophy for Sandy and Bob Lundberg of South Carolina, with two each of five varieties (all blooms shown separately in individual containers), were 'Autumn Splendor', 'Bella Via', 'Patriot's Dream', 'Tiffany Lynn', and 'Violet Mist'. There are also classes with trophies from J. Benjamin Williams available to those who wish to exhibit Mini-Floras at many local shows. In the United Kingdom the 2001 Royal National Rose Society's International Show of Miniature Roses saw the American-bred 'Cachet' win for Californian exhibitor and former president of the American Rose Society, Dr. Tommy Cairns, and partner Luis Desamero.

The expansion of these classes will continue apace. Initially, the awards were for individual blooms with the high-pointed, standard hybrid tea-style bloom. But there is room for many other classes featuring decorative form, using either floribunda-or grandiflora-style Mini-Floras, where the looser and more floriferous sprays can be seen to advantage.

Some brief advice for taking your roses to a show. Cut blooms as soon as they are ready in the garden, place them in warm water and take away any dirt or dust that may have accumulated on them before placing them in your carrying container. The container should have a 50-50 mixture of water and a fizzy soft drink at the bottom; a 50-50 solution of lemon-lime soda and water is often recommended as it is acidic and provides needed sugar. My own personal mix is a soluble aspirin and a little sugar, which seems to work for me but is often decried by experts. Floral preservatives in the water do help in extending the life of your cut Mini-Floras; try *Floralife, Rogard* or *Chrysal* in this regard. You can keep the cut blooms in a fridge for a number of days at 34 to 35 degrees. Cover the container as tightly as possible, only opening it to quickly add fresh blooms. The best way is to cut the blooms the day of the show and bring them along in water.

The perfect hybrid tea-type bloom will be half to three-quarters open. Rosette or floribunda-type shapes, which naturally open fully, should have stamens of fresh color, not dark and aging. The blooms and stem should be in proportion; avoid a thick stem and a small bloom or a tiny stem and a big bloom.

If you are entering a spray instead of an individual bloom, the only difference is that the buds should be left on the stem (on individual blooms—one bloom per stem entries—do not leave the side buds). Blooms should be fairly open and showing color. If you can have them all fresh and at the same stage you are likely

'Patriot's Dream', MinFl

53

'House Beautiful', MinFl

to have a winner.

Crooked stems are likely to lose points.

Remember these hints: arrive early, know your schedule and don't be rushed. I know some people who wouldn't think it was a show unless they were running madly about—leading exhibitors rarely do.

When you have your entry ready, put it in its place or ask for assistance.

There is no doubt that showing is a great hobby. The Mini-Flora can be your way to success, and remember that because of their great production of blooms, you don't need a garden full of plants to succeed. The flowers cut judiciously from a single container-grown plant can easily be winners.

Remember that you are not just taking your roses to the show for a personal ego boost (although I will never deny that this motive must be part of the scheme), you are taking them so someone who has never grown a rose will be encouraged to go out and try it. You are also bringing brightness and knowledge into other people's lives. That is what rose shows are for.

* The details given here are necessarily brief. For a far more detailed and expert work on exhibiting, search out a book called *Showing Good Roses (A Complete Exhibitor's Guide)* by Robert B. Martin Jr. (published by RoseShow.com). This is everything you ever wanted to know about showing roses but didn't know what to ask.

Here for a smile (I hope) is my own "Ode to a Rose Show"
This is the tale of exhibitor Joe
Getting his roses ready to show,
He looked 'round his garden with obvious glee
"I've never had better, not ever." said he.
So he cut them in three's and he cut them in two's
He cut all the reds and quite a few blues,
And before evening was out Joe was quite tight
Never had he seen such a wonderful sight.

Also preparing was rosarian Fred
Who looked round his garden with a terrible dread
All he could see were a few battered flowers
Beaten to death by hailstones and showers.
Could he cut one or with luck cut two?
So very unhappy he hadn't a clue
Then he went off to bed still filled with dread
That tomorrow he might be better off dead.

But Joe was ecstatic and sat up all night
Labeling and looking at his blooms, oh so bright.
He dressed and he tied them and gazed full of pride
"They're the best bloomin' blooms in the whole world," he cried.

He packed them all up without even a yawn
And headed for town at the first sight of dawn
And there in the hall surrounded by blooms,
He laughed at poor Fred and his obvious gloom.
The roses went up and the judges came down
To niggle and jiggle and chuckle and frown,
Two exhibits stood out above all the rest
There was Fred's, there was Joe's, put up to the test.

Oh, Joe's they were lovely, so big and so bold
They must be the winner - then, lo and behold
A judge had knelt down 'fore a Red Devil so fine
And he let out a gasp, "It's tied up with twine!"

An acre of string - well, hardly that much
But a piece long enough to cause a great hush,

'Cachet', MinFl

Indeed it was Joe's bloom all trussed up and tied
And a championship dream, at that moment, died.
Fred was the winner, with delight and surprise
He went to the stage and collected his prize.

The moral of this is
never be rude
To the other man's roses
no matter how crude.

True story! Yes, I was the Joe in the story...I did leave a piece of
wool tying up my roses, and they were disqualified as the wool
was foreign matter!

'Alice Faye', Min

'Ruffian', MinFl

'High Life', Min

'Orange Kordana', Min

Chapter 9
Pests And Diseases

When a human gets a touch of the flu there is an immediate move to get a tablet to fix it. But when a rose gets a touch of mildew or blackspot or some other trouble, it is disaster! Why not use the human remedy and give it a little help to make it better?

A lot has been made over the years about "the trouble with roses." The world's greatest flower has been the subject of unwarranted and unmerited comments. It has been denigrated, disparaged and maligned over something that is no more than a cold in the head for humans. Most insect pests can be taken care of with a finger and thumb to demolish them, and while it is true that in most climates the occasional use of chemical fungicides is essential to successful rose culture, much of the talk about roses being disease prone is excessive. It is often mentioned as if it was a fatal flaw in rose makeup. The truth is diseases are neither catastrophic, critical nor crucial. Indeed, in some climates roses can be grown without chemical fungicides. Not all roses, of course, but where one misbehaves you will find that it is simply a minor flaw that is no worse than any of the troubles that generally strike gardens and plants. And it is no worse than most plant diseases insofar as it is possible to clean it up with very little effort.

"The trade, plus garden magazines and the press, must teach the gardening public to live with some mildew, spider mites or whatever," says Elsa Spek of Jan Spek Rosen in Holland. "There are many ornamentals and shrubs that also get diseases and nobody seems to bother about them."

A survey among rose purchasers in Australia showed that disease consideration was never a factor for them when it came to buying a rosebush. Customers didn't ask if the rose was susceptible to anything; to them the rose was a beautiful impulse buy. If the plant looked good—with or without flowers—then it was purchased.

There will, no doubt, be those who will want to continue to damn the rose because of some very minor infringements of the good growth code, but when figures are looked at, it will be found that modern roses are far better than ever in this regard. Looked at side by side with roses of even 30 years ago, the current crop

'Conundrum' MinFl

'Double Gold' MinFl

of varieties is way ahead of the older ones. And the Mini-Floras have been bred with the whole idea of roses having a better future. They are positively stronger in their ability to withstand all the usual rose diseases.

All over the world, breeders have the dream of producing more disease resistant roses at the top of their lists.

English breeder Chris Warner (who is responsible for many new climbing miniatures) had a discussion recently with his German counterpart Reinhardt Noack (from the family that bred the "Flower Carpet" ground cover roses of great disease resistance) in which both agreed that health was their number one requirement in all roses, and this was qualified by "total health" which, translated to rose growing, means bushes that do not generally fall victim to blackspot and mildew and grow with ease and vitality. This is a wish that has been with rose enthusiasts and breeders down the years, but until that day is reached all gardeners should remember that old adage that prevention is better than cure. I put it on a par with getting my annual flu inoculation before the influenza season begins. Neglect of your roses (or your own health) will always encourage trouble. Anticipate the problem early on and then success is not far away.

Getting the balance right is what nature calls for. Once that is established, we can all live in harmony. The main message is that roses that are well fed and watered will be helped by human hand to withstand the nastier forces of nature. This doesn't mean you have to run out every other day with a bucket of water and douse the plants, nor does it mean you have to feed them every week. Balance is the word to remember.

Spraying is something that is still a contentious area of gardening. What every gardener looks for is a system that will keep the situation under control and will not ruin the bank balance or the environment. There are two sets of gardeners here: those who will panic and over-spray, and the others who will do nothing. You can see the difference all around you.

I begin the season by spraying with a fungicide as soon as the first foliage emerges and I follow up with a second spray about two weeks later. This puts the roses in good heart. The *maximum* you will need to spray is once a month. After that, to do it more often is like giving a child a lollipop every Saturday morning, upon which the child then expects it to be delivered. Roses are the same. Spray them too often and they come to expect it.

In matters of spraying, some are lucky and some are not. In the climatic conditions of southern California, they laugh at the thought of fungicidal spraying, but not everyone can be so fortunate. Many people like to wait until they see the first signs of blackspot before spraying, but that defeats the purpose. Preventative spraying is far more effective, as it will take weeks to eradicate established disease, and during this time the spores have already have had a great time spreading to other foliage. Preventative action will have wiped out that spore before it has a chance to grow into a larger colony.

Remember to cover all the foliage with the spray; any less only invites trouble. Don't spray in strong sunshine—it can burn the foliage—nor in rainy conditions, as all sprays need a couple of hours to become effective.

This routine will help keep your roses in top order. To make sure you do the same for yourself, remember that all sprays, if handled carelessly, can be dangerous to humans, animals and the environment.

'Flower Power' MinFl

'Happy Times' MinFl

Some Basic Rules:

•If there has been a dry period, water all roses thoroughly the day before you spray. This supplies moisture to the plants so they won't have to rely on the liquid content of the spray material.

•Dress appropriately when spraying by wearing rubber gloves, long sleeves, long trousers, a facemask and a hat.

•Avoid fumes and powder drift by mixing your sprays in a well-ventilated area. Do not mix outdoors or carry out spraying on windy days when the drift might fall on you, your neighbor or other plants.

•Fill the spray tank with the required amount of water, then add the spray mixture. If you put the spray mixture in first it could result in the material staying at the bottom of the tank and not mixing to the correct dilution.

•Spray all bushes until they begin to drip.

•Only spray for insects when you see them in the garden. The gardener who visits with his roses often will see just what needs doing and can put a stop to a swarm with a deft finger and thumb to eliminate the early visitors.

•Remember that wishful thinking and hindsight have never been parts of a good garden program.

'Hand in Hand', MinFl

'Pink Pirouette', MinFl

'Romantic Palace', MinFl

'Laura', MinFl

'Pinocchio', MiniFl

Chapter 10
Troubleshooter Guide

A listing of problems you may meet in your gardening life. And these are not confined to just roses; most gardens have their problems. However, I have been growing roses for almost half a century, and I have never found anyone who has experienced all these things. So take heart and just remember to look ahead, and look often.

The following chapter is adapted from one of my earlier books: *Miniature Roses – for Home and Garden.*

Plants are slow to start

Check to see if they have been planted loosely; if the plant moves easily, push the soil tighter around the neck. Wind rocking after planting will loosen bushes that may have been planted firmly earlier on. If an older plant seems to be loose where it has been well established, look for a bug at the roots. It could be ants, chafer grubs or a weevil. Other likely causes of slow starting include:

• A waterlogged site, which is as bad as a site that is too dry; the roots cannot survive therein.

• Use of fresh manure at planting time. Manure should be allowed to sit for a few months at least, and even then should be kept away from direct contact with the roots.

• Roots that have dried out by planting time. Always soak new bushes for 24 hours before planting and then puddle them in. If there is a spell of dry weather after planting, be sure the bushes are carefully monitored for their water needs.

Weevils and chafer grubs

These can multiply very quickly. In the open, garden spraying or dusting with a suitable insecticide should be done in midsummer. In the glasshouse, the likelihood is that, from mid-winter onward, these pests are hard at work and can be found at all stages of development: eggs, larvae and adults. Soil should be sterilized before repotting, and this can be done in a number of ways. The most accepted way is to steam clean it (you can buy special containers that operate on electrical current). Another method is

'Emily Louise', MiniFl

'Graceland', MiniFl

to pour boiling water right through the soil, but if you have a lot of soil you need a lot of water to maintain the heat all the way through. There are also soil fumigants that can be purchased, *but these should be used with the greatest of care*. Once you have been bothered by these nasties, you must keep watch out and even anticipate a re-infestation. Be extra careful of potted plants brought in from an outside source.

Leggy plants with few blooms

They haven't been getting enough sun, or possibly enough food. Check for a sunny position; they need six hours sun a day if possible. If the problem is a lack of feeding, give them a root feeding with a special rose fertilizer, as well as additional foliar feedings. Small doses are better than a banquet.

Buds fail to open or fall off before they reach full color stage

This is something you can't really do a lot about, as the weather is nearly always the cause, particularly cool nights, little sun and cold winds. Heavy rain often makes buds sodden and they turn into a brown mess. It is best to cut blooms early in wet weather and enjoy them indoors. This also gives the plant a chance to set about producing a new set of blooms quickly. Do make sure that there isn't an attack of aphids around the site because they too can cause all sorts of problems on the blooms, as well as the stems (aphids are dealt with specifically later). Thrips can also be a problem; these are sucking insects, and they love a bloom that is just about to open, usually ones you have planned on being a show winner! Brown marks, stains and distortions around the petal edges are indications of thrips. The normal garden insecticide doesn't work here, and you will have to name your pest specifically when you visit a garden center to get a deterrent. One thing in favor of the Mini-Floras is that thrips seem to avoid the blooms far more than they do on bigger roses.

The presence of the rose midge can also cause blooms to be distorted or fail to open, causing both buds and leaves to turn black and die. The midge is a tiny brown or red insect that lays its eggs on the rose, where the grubs can feed on the buds and leaves. While thrips are again more serious on larger roses than on Mini-Floras, they will attack if given a chance. Spray once a week, but if the buds have become too infected for a spray to do any good, it is best to cut the bloom off and let the bush get on with producing some more.

Mottled, yellow, tinted or badly discolored foliage

Don't panic. If the plant is otherwise well and healthy looking, it may be that light colorings are just part of its makeup. But when lack of color appears with stunted leaves that fall easily, accompanied by an unhappy bush, then you know you have problems. Yellowing of the leaves, especially the young ones, denotes an iron shortage, too much lime, an excess of phosphoric acid or manganese, too much moisture or damage to the root system. Avoid over-liming, use a chelate of iron such as *Sequestrene*, and then follow some days later with a water soluble fertilizer. All other problems such as nitrogen deficiency (small pale-green leaves, often with red spots, early leaf fall), potash shortage (usually seen in sandy soils when blooms are undersized and foliage has brown, brittle margins) and phosphate shortage (stunted plants, small leaves with purplish tints) can be cured by the application of a well-balanced rose fertilizer used according to the manufacturer's instructions.

Leaves, stalks and stems are distorted and dying back

This is often the result of a weed killer or herbicide spray drifting in over the small roses, which are more liable to damage than larger ones since they are closer to the ground. Cut off the affected parts and the plant should quickly begin to recover. Remember that a container used for weed killer should never be used for any other spraying operation.

White, green, red or brown insects are invading the stems and buds

These are aphids, probably the most persistent of all rose pests. They suck the most tender parts of the rose, taking away all the nourishment. They also increase a hundredfold overnight and continue to reproduce. Definitely a pest to clear away quickly! There are two sorts of insecticides that can be used to control them—one is a contact spray that kills off the adult aphid, the other is a systemic spray that goes into the plant, kills off the adults, and stays long enough in the plant to kill off the next generations too. Some brands contain both contact and systemic

'Harm Saville', MiniFl

'Jerry Lynn', MiniFl

'Luscious Lucy', MiniFl

types and are particularly useful in halting a sudden attack, such as can build up on plants growing against a warm wall or fence. A sticky secretion or a white mass of little pieces around a plant is also an indication that you have aphids somewhere about. Keeping an eye out for them will enable you to stay in control. If you object to the use of sprays and have only a few bushes, the old-fashioned finger-and-thumb method will work. A less gory method, often suggested as a variation to the ordinary spraying program, is to wash the affected stems with soap and water. Unfortunately, it doesn't work. It does knock the aphids off, but the little bugs recover after a minute or so and when they are sure that no other flood is coming their way, they just shake themselves off and start scrambling up the rose again! Maybe a few lie dead but they are the unlucky minority. I once tried bringing in a big collection of ladybugs to control the aphids, which they did for a while. But as soon as their food was gone the ladybugs took wing and proceeded to do the work for my neighbors, and by the end of the summer there were very few ladybugs in the area. They had obviously winged off to pastures where the prospects were better. But if you are a believer in their effectiveness, don't let me stop you.

Chewed leaves or buds

The caterpillar, which can appear in many forms, may be the culprit. Fortunately this is another visitor that mainly troubles the big roses and is not too keen on the little Mini-Floras, which fail to give the larvae adequate cover. Watch for rolled up leaves and then pick off individual pests. Children have wonderful eyes for these—especially if they get a monetary reward for every one captured. They are then transported (the caterpillars, not the children) to a meadow nearby where they can continue with their evolution.

Leaves spotted gray, brown, red or yellow; leaf fall

Don't mistake this for blackspot. It is likely to be red spider mite, a tiny spider-like sucking arachnid that arrives when the weather is hot and humid and keeps out of sight on the underside of the leaves. A keen eye will know when it's there. It is a very serious pest in greenhouses. Spider mites have built up quite an immunity to many miticidal sprays, so the gardener may have to try a number before finding one that is really effective. A fine jet with very good pressure is needed when spraying, which should be done every seven days to make sure that you clean away any new hatchings that emerge.

Large circular holes in the leaves and blooms

This is the work of the Japanese beetle, whose depredations are spreading across America and other parts of the world. It is the worst and *the ugliest* beetle of all. Look for a half-inch long body, metallic green with copper-brown wings. Hand pick any specimens from the plants and drop them into a container of kerosene. My only knowledge of them has been in other people's gardens (along the east coast of the United States), but I have seen blooms turned over and the dreaded beetles falling out in piles.

White, frothy spittle on shoots

This is a cuckoo-spit or froghopper, sometimes called a spittlebug in America, which appears early in the year. Leave it there and you will eventually find distorted shoots. If you have only a few roses, then the finger-and-thumb exercise of squashing the little greenish bug inside the spittle will be effective; if not, then a good insecticide used forcibly on the spittle will do the trick.

Regular-shaped holes at the sides of leaves

Caused by a bee called the leaf cutter. Control is not really necessary, the bee may just be passing by, but if the cutting becomes persistent, then you must search out the nest and destroy it.

'Memphis King', MiniFl

Skeletonized areas of foliage

Areas on the leaves turn gray or brown and all greenery seems to be eaten away, leaving only the veins. This is the work of the rose slug, a greenish-yellow grub seen on the leaf surface. A systemic insecticide will do the trick.

Holes in the flower bud

Inside the hole you will probably find a small brown maggot known as the totrix moth. If it isn't inside the bud, look around for a curled-up leaf, and you will find it in temporary residence there. Pick off the affected buds and you won't have trouble, but

'Moonlight Scentsation', MiniFl

'Peach Delight', MiniFl

if the damage looks like too much to cope with in this way, you will have to turn to one of the sprays that eliminate caterpillars.

Dark spots on leaves with a surrounding yellow area; leaves turning yellow and falling off

This is almost surely blackspot disease. Once almost unknown in industrial areas, it is now to be found just about everywhere since clean air laws have become more rigidly enforced. It starts as early as the first buds of spring, and if allowed to keep going will result in a plant with small, undernourished blooms and no foliage. Spray regularly with one of the many new and very effective systemic fungicides. Pick off diseased leaves and keep a watchful eye for the starter spots. When the weather is wet and warm, you have the ideal situation for the disease to grow. A good idea is to alternate your spray materials to avoid the spores becoming resistant to any given one.

White or gray powdery substance on leaves and stems; leaves curling up

This is mildew, the powdery variety, and the conditions that bring it on are cool nights, humid days and little rain. It is a summer trouble, when you are not expecting such things to happen. Mildew is regarded by many as the most widespread of rose diseases, although more resistant varieties of roses are arriving on the market all the time. If your plants are susceptible, then a look at where they are planted (too close to a wall, where roots are dry and there is little ventilation, for example) will often reveal the cause of the problem. A well-fed and cared for plant will have a better chance of resisting the problem. Spray immediately when the disease appears, and if the soil is dry, water well. These days, you will find that the same fungicide can control both blackspot and mildew, so a regular walk among your roses is the way to success.

Rusty orange-like swellings appearing at first under the leaf and then coming through the top surface

The old killer, rust, is seen early in summer and must be taken in hand immediately. A potassium shortage encourages the disease, but adding potash to the soil won't help if the disease is already there. There are sprays that are quite effective against all three major diseases: rust, mildew and blackspot. Don't always blame the rose; some gardens harbor pockets of rust that will affect varieties that would have remained healthy elsewhere.

Rough, tumor-like growths near the roots

These are caused by crown gall, a disease that enters wounds made by digging or hoeing. It won't cause a great deal of harm on stems but, like every disease, is better done away with. Cut the galls off with a sharp knife and treat the wound with a sealant. Also disinfect your secateurs or knife. If the galls appear on the roots the problem is more serious and it is likely that the whole plant will die unless you are ruthless; take it up immediately and cut out the bad parts.

Brown or sunken area along the stem

The bark looks as though it has been cut away and a disease has broken through. It is known as canker, and it is often caused by damage while gardening or by bugs eating away at the outer bark. It will spread and eventually encircle the stem, killing all wood above it. This is one to watch for in outdoor-grown Mini-Floras because the little ones can easily be damaged while you are hoeing or working the soil around them. Care is the first method of prevention, but if the canker gets big, you may as well cut it out and burn the affected wood. When such diseased areas are found in early spring, prune to a good bud below. Also clean the secateurs in disinfectant before using them again.

Frightened off by all of this? Don't be! The majority of rose growers will not have experienced anywhere near the greater part of these troubles. Remember my earlier advice that "Anticipation and Prevention" should be the slogan for the gardener.

'Snow Hit', MiniFl

'Scarlet Patio', MiniFl

'Sugar Baby', Min

Chapter 11
A Rose of Your Very Own

Cherishing dreamers is vital to the world of horticulture. Without their imagination there would be nothing. No great new roses to whet our lives and imaginations.

"It has been given to the hand of man to help beautify the garden of the Lord." These words were attributed to a pope many years ago when he was addressing a group of rose breeders. And man has, I believe, done his part with distinction. No matter where your particular alliance lies, whether it be with old or modern roses, man has done wondrous things with them. There has been no holding back on the paths that have been opened for the world's gardens with roses of every shade, shape and hue available to everyone, everywhere.

I once wrote that being a hybridizer is akin to being a juggler. You have to keep all the objects in the air and then introduce some more. If modern breeders weren't all juggling to produce another great rose, wouldn't that be a major surprise? Today there is a wonderful concoction of silhouettes, shapes and forms with roses, producing blooms of every description that are as magical (and even, dare I say, more so) as any blooms of any other flower that ever graced this earth.

This has been so for hundreds of years, with man introducing wonderful tea roses, hybrid perpetuals, hybrid musks, bourbons, centifolias—oh, the list is thankfully endless. In following that path, they discovered roses with many differences and variations to the original. That same thing is with us today. The huge variety of shapes, colors and growth habits staggers belief and is equal to anything produced before them.

The rose world is not singular. It is a superlative collection of everything the earliest roses passed on to be organized by the hand of man—with, no doubt, great assistance from a higher place. We should never knock the hybridizer who goes searching for that compelling (if often elusive) perfection.

You don't have to be a professional hybridizer to become one of those who have produced some little spark of beauty in this great collection

The story of Herb Zipper, a chemist from Baldwin, NY, who

a

began breeding roses as a hobby in 1982, proves this. This was the time when miniatures were the invasive ones on the market, but he had a different image for his roses. He wanted to increase gardeners' vision of what the rose world could be. Being purely an amateur, his livelihood was not dependent on rose sales or royalties, so he decided to be a little more adventurous.

b

"For a while I followed along the path of such breeders of miniatures as Harm Saville, Nelson Jolly, Ernie Schwartz and others of the time. It was fun, but if you look at the heritage of many of the minis of that era, they were, for the most part, quite similar (Ralph Moore's were different). So I looked at roses like 'Tamango', a red floribunda from Meilland in France, 'Sparrieshoop', a light pink shrub from Kordes in Germany, plus the different roses bred by Griffith Buck of Iowa, and decided that these would be part of my program.

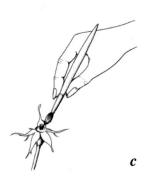

c

"I bred a lot of nice roses from these but few wanted them, mainly because there was no place among the exhibition classes for them. However, my small buying public loved them. But no one else wanted them, so the result was that most of the seedlings went into the compost pile.

"Along the way I came up with a number of what would now be called 'mini-Austins.' These were roses with an old-fashioned look and form—the sort that made David Austin and his English roses such a success. But no one wanted them so they were thrown out too. Now every time we see Austin roses, I needle my wife telling her we could have had our own line of 'mini-Americana' roses."

d

His persistence paid off, and now Zipper's too-big-to-be-minis and too-small-to-be-anything-else roses have found their place by winning top awards on the show bench. Among these are 'Love Note', 'Night Music', 'Bella Via' and 'Raspberry Ice'. Now his ambition is to name a rose in honor and memory for his daughter Julie Lynne, who was lost in the Twin Towers disaster of 9/11. He wants it to be one of his best ever.

e

That is the great thing about breeding roses—you can produce very good and totally new roses without having access to anything more than a dream. Over the years I have recommended that anyone with a love of plants should try breeding some of their own varieties. And these words have not fallen on deaf ears. One great friend of mine, David Kenny, flatters me that it was my enthusiasm that brought him into hybridizing. Today he has many roses that carry his name as the breeder, including one very good Mini-Flora, 'Riverdance'. It is a good thing he didn't take the professionals' advice that you have one chance in eight million of getting a good rose from your hybridizing. Most amateurs should remember the other side of the equation: that you can plant two seeds and they could turn out two good roses.

I do a little hybridizing, but I must say that my successes *f* cover a multitude of blunders. Every year I have a few hundred seeds that may result in about 100 seedlings, very seldom any more than that. I do it all in a 12 foot x 8 foot greenhouse — just about big enough to turn around in when there are plants growing there. But from that I have produced a great number of seedlings that are grown in my own garden; some of them are now on sale in the United States, and more are expected in the next few years.

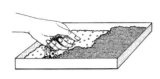

When it comes to providing magical moments, there is nothing quite like the sight of the first of the new rose seedlings breaking *g* through the soil. Anne-Sophie Rondeau wrote in her book *The Quest for the Black Rose:*

"In the first days of spring, the rose breeders hardly sleep at all. Is it due to the full moon? No, it is simply the time when roses are born. Just after the lambs at Easter. The moment so eagerly awaited and which, in the space of a few weeks, helps forget all the painstaking work, the discouragement about crossings, the anguish as to whether anything will result, the constant eradicating of invading weeds, insects and other pests...."

Two little ears sprout up, and in about two weeks the first real *h* rose foliage is discernible, followed in another few weeks by the first little flower. The sooner you can get the crosses made, the better chance there is of them reaching maturity. In about a year you can have your very own seedling blooming and hopefully ready to carry your own piece of glory into history.

The simple method for hybridizing is to have two different varieties, preferably growing in pots. They should come into bloom at the same time. In most climates you will need some cover for the success of this operation. Sun and heat are the immediate requirements. When your two plants come into bloom just move pollen from one to the other and vice versa, and you are on the way to creating a rose of your very own. There are no rules about the roses that you select as parents, but the best advice *i*

'Velvet Cloak', Min

is "breed from the best to the best and hope for the best." This is what horse breeders tell each other, and it is a rule that is repeated in the plant world. When the parent flowers are at the one-quarter open stage, gently remove all the petals, making sure you do not leave any petal pieces behind. Try this out on any bloom at any time so you know what the particular parts of the rose bloom are. Take away all the anthers (these surround the stigma or reproductive parts of the bloom) using either a small pair of scissors or tweezers. This is the pollen (the male part of the reproductive system); save it on a sheet of paper and mark the name at the top. Your second rose, which may be used as a mother (seed producer) or father (pollen parent), should be prepared in the same way. Don't mix the pollen; place the separate sheets of paper holding it in a fridge overnight. It will keep much longer that way, but if kept for too long in the cold atmosphere it will need a day or so to regenerate itself when taken into the warmth. You will know that the pollen is ready when you gently shake the paper and see a yellow mustard-like deposit. Transfer the pollen of rose #1 onto the stigma of rose #2 by using your index finger (or a small brush) and vice versa. Tie a small tag on the stems that tells you which roses you have crossed. If the cross-pollination takes place in a greenhouse there is no need to cover the rose, but if you do it in the open you will need to place a small paper cone over the head.

Leave the roses alone after the pollen has been transferred. Hopefully they will develop into pods carrying viable seeds. These pods or hips will take about 12 weeks to ripen.

After that, the most widely used system is to open the hips individually and give the seeds the water test: put them in a cupful of water and those that sink are fertile; many hybridizers throw away the floaters, but I keep them. The surviving seeds are then wrapped in a small piece of damp kitchen paper towel, placed inside a small plastic baggie and put away in the bottom of the fridge, all clearly labeled with the name of the cross. They are left in the vegetable compartment of the fridge for about six weeks. However, there is an alternative method. Just when the pods have ripened, take out the seeds and plant them immediately. This seems to have no adverse effect on them and most will germinate quickly. I have reached a personal conclusion over many years that rose seeds will grow just about anywhere—eventually. But to give them the best start find a good potting mix (some companies actually sell small starter bags). Mix in a little perlite to allow the roots to breathe. Never soak this potting mix, just keep it gently moist. Under-soil heating produces germination quicker, but I have never bothered with that, and in time the seeds have emerged quite happily.

In a matter of weeks the first seeds should be showing through the soil. Two little leaves like rabbits' ears appear first, and are eventually followed by the true rose leaves. I have found that seeds planted in January will be in flower in March, April and May. If the seed trays are deep enough—I have found that the best are 9 inches deep — the plants can be left in them to flower. If the trays are the normal 2 to 3 inches deep, the seedlings should be lifted as soon as the first two leaves have established themselves and placed in small pots with a good potting mixture. Always lift the seedlings by the leaves, as the slightest pressure can damage the tiny stem growth. This is personal advice, since I have seen Ralph Moore grow all his seedlings until their second flowering in trays 2 inches deep.

Now you have your own roses, and all you have to do is wait and see how good they are. Give them time to see how they develop. Do not throw them away until you are sure there is no hope for them, because even the most unpromising roses are beautiful in their own ways.

If you want to transfer a more mature plant at any stage after it has become established (as opposed to a very new seedling), lift gently and place it in a mist tray with heat and constant misting for a week or so. Grow it for a year or two before you make a decision about keeping it. Do not try to take cuttings from a small plant or you may lose it. In its second summer, it should be strong enough to be propagated. It may not put you in the same league as the masters, but who cares; this is a personal moment of glory! In my own case, if I can produce just one rose that will bring a smile to someone's face, then I have justified well the time I have spent on my hobby.

To quote California resident, Canadian-born rose hybridizer Jerry Twomey: "The only record you leave behind you here on this earth is that you have contributed a little—in my case some beauty—to the world."

* If you would like to know more about hybridizing, contact the

'Gossamer Wings', S

Rose Hybridizer's Association, c/o Treasurer Larry Peterson, 2345 Wheaton Road, Horseheads, NY 14845, or in the United Kingdom, the Amateur Rose Breeders Association, c/o Secretary Derek Everitt, 48 Shrewsbury Fields, Shifnal, Shropshire TF11 8AN. U.K.

'Charismatic', MinFl

'Solar Flair', MinFl

'Bloomsday', Fl

Chapter 12

My Own Seedlings

I have been writing, breeding, dreaming about roses for more than 40 years. My attitude, my belief in them remains resolute, inflexible and constant. They are the obsession of my life—and isn't it a gentle one? Roses are a simple obsession of gentle happiness that breathe with our lives and express true beauty. They are love, romance, excitement. And they aren't alcoholic, they aren't fattening, they aren't immoral.

Over the years I have hybridized many, many seedlings. They are scattered all over my garden where they either live with me and defeat all that nature throws at them, or else disappear to little rose heaven.

It all began when I came in one afternoon and found our eldest son (also a Sean) putting some pollen on another bloom. I asked him what he was doing and he told me that I had been talking of this for so long without doing anything about it and that he had decided to start me off! So I started…and that was the beginning of a wonderful road.

Then one very lucky day I met a man named Jerry Justice who was just starting a miniature rose nursery near Portland, OR. At that time I had never had a seedling introduced, so when I mentioned this to him he suggested that I send some on for trials.

I knew this had to be right for me because I have been very lucky in roses and because two previous friends were named Jerry. So this was a sign. And very soon Justice wrote me that one of the first to bloom had enchanted him. I had named it 'You 'n' Me'. When introducing it, he wrote: "A lightly perfumed performer that can't seem to decide what color it really wants to be. You'll see pure white, white with apricot shading and occasionally soft pink on the same bush, sometimes on the same day. All the buds are sharply pointed and the foliage is a leathery, dark green with sharply serrated edges."

And that is how it all began. After that, for a long number of years, Justice introduced many of my roses. When he died I was shattered, not because of my roses, but because a great friend had passed on.

I thought little more about marketing my roses until one day

I contacted Paul Zimmerman of Ashdown Roses to see if he was interested in any of them. Zimmerman picked up the baton for me, eventually doing me the great honor of not just cataloging my roses, but also planting a garden in my name at his nursery in South Carolina.

Although I didn't know it then, I already had a fan in the Ashdown Roses company. Her name is Trish Walsh, and she had been collecting my roses over the years. Now she too got involved, and started to try to trace all my roses that had been introduced, a task at which she has been phenomenally successful.

You might think that I would have been businesslike, or conscientious enough to make sure that all my own roses would be planted in my own garden. Unfortunately my garden is so small that it just was not possible.

And, of course, like every other hybridizer, I had many roses with no place to go in the classifications, roses that now would be easily accommodated in the Mini-Flora group. Even today some of my roses that I registered as miniatures should be re-classified as Mini-Floras. It is high on my list of things to do.

I never knowingly "threw out" any seedlings — big, small or indifferent. I just took them on my walks around the countryside close to home and slipped them in the hedgerows. Anne-Sophie Rondeau wrote about this penchant of mine in *The Quest for the Black Rose*: "He plants them here and there, in the hollow of a hedge, on the edge of a field, these seedlings of roses he cannot keep. And they live their own lives or die under the hooves of the oxen, the teeth of a chainsaw or the jaws of harmful insects. They may also survive and do more than survive, they blossom, inspire joy in the eyes of passers-by, a petal of hope in the beauty of the world."

All of my roses carry the "code letters"—the first three letters of the code name—of SEA; for example, the code name of 'Admirable' is **SEArodney**. (In this case, the rest of the name derives from 'Admiral Rodney', one of the parents). Using the first three letters of my name (Sean) seemed the easy way out as "MAC" was already claimed by Sam McGredy. It was a simple move and was easy to follow through. In a way it was sort of like leaving my isolation behind, as there were no other rose breeders near me. It was a companionship thing, and I could always be with my rose family when I was otherwise alone in the garden.

Here then is a list of some of my roses; I hope you enjoy them.

'Admirable' Mini — Ivory buds accented with lots of pink. One of my most fragrant creations. Large 3-inch blooms, borne singly on long stems.

'Admirable', Min

'Ain't Misbehavin'' Mini — Five very dark red petals surround the bright yellow stamens to produce a classic single.

'Alice Faye' Mini — A lovely bicolor named for a great film musical actress. She has grown up for me since it began and can reach 2.5 feet high.

'Anneli' MinFl — A pretty bicolor seedling that was found by my son Ronan among roses that he collected for me from the Jerry Justice fields in Oregon after the owner's death.

'Brightness', Min

'Blushing Groom' Mini* — White blooms with a mild fragrance.

'Brightness' Mini — Named for a novel written by our son Colum. Bright creamy yellow blooms with touches of pink at the edges.

'Canoodling' Mini — A sister seedling of 'San Francisco Sunset', but distinguished by interesting yellow stripes through the petals. A very good bush.

'Canoodling', MiniFl

'Capricious' Mini* — Light pink, long-lasting, exhibition-form blooms, coming mostly one to a stem.

'Ciana Rose' Mini — Pink, old-fashioned-style blooms on a continually flowering plant.

'Colette Pappin Glynn' Mini — A low-growing yellow with superb, glossy foliage. Great for containers.

'Convivial' Cl. Mini* — Apricot blooms

'Crazy Dottie' Mini — Loaded with soft orange blooms that close their five petals at night to shade their yellow eyes. A great

'Ciana Rose', Min

'Collette Pappin Glynn', Min

'Crazy Dottie', Min

'Cupid's Mark', Min

'Dreamcatcher', Cl Min

'Dreamcoat', Cl Min

exhibition single when you learn how to predict its flower opening. Named for a friend in California who herself selected the name. Hardy and nearly impervious to diseases.

'Cupid's Mark' Mini — Single blooms, striped in shades of pink.

'Dancer' Mini — Mauve blooms on a plant that was again named for a son's novel.

'Darby O'Gill' Mini — Orange and white striped blooms on a little plant named for the famous film leprechaun.

'Dark Mirage' Mini — High centered, maroon red blooms with a dark shadow at the base.

'Different Charm' Mini — Orange-red blooms with a lighter reverse. Blooms are slightly fragrant, heavily petalled in a mushroom-like shape.

'Dreamcatcher' CL Mini — Red and white striped miniature climber. Deserves a sunny spot and a trellis that will allow it to climb.

'Dreamcoat' CL Mini — Virtually a miniature clone of its pollen parent, 'Joseph's Coat'. Yellow florets that pick up lipstick red shading as they open.

'Elizabeth Munn' Mini — Pink blooms on a very floriferous plant.

'Fair Eva' Mini —Soft pink, well shaped blooms on a short, shrubby plant.

'Flower Basket' Mini — A colorful groundcover or hanging basket variety with "hand-painted" red and white flowers and a thick mass of dark green foliage.

'Frauenfelder' Mini — White blooms with orange-yellow centers.

'Glad Eye' Mini* — Low-petalled, red blooms with yellow centers, forming in small clusters on a short, compact plant.

'Gold Country' MinFl — A yellow, beautifully shaped bloom. I only wish it would grow better! Named for a California Rose Society of which I am delighted to be an Honorary Life Member.

'Flower Basket', Min

'High Life' Mini — High-centered, deep pinkish-red petals reversed with chalk white that are about 3 inches across when open. Habit is upright.

'In the Mood' Mini — A subdued bloom of soft mauve and yellow stripes. Most attractive at the fully open stage. Hardy and resistant plant.

'Irish Heartbreaker' Mini — Named by the Justice family, so I had nothing to do with it! It is almost a climbing rose (but slow and low) with dark red blooms.

'Frauenfelder', Min

'Isabella Cara' Mini — A shrubby plant bearing white blooms with a suggestion of pink.

'Jazz Dancer' (Twinkletoes) Mini — Orange and yellow blooms that are at their best when fully open.

'Kiss Me Quick' Mini** — Full, light pink blooms with a mild fragrance on a medium-sized plant.

'Gold Country', MiniFl

'Kiss 'n' Tell' Mini? — Upright plant habit to about 3 feet, covered with urn shaped, apricot blossoms. Does well even when neglected! I had a friend who was very ill in the hospital and requested two flowers of this rose, "because with a name like that you must have two blooms."

'Kiss the Bride' Mini — Pure white buds opening to blooms borne in clusters of five or more, each about an inch across. Great for small bouquets.

'Knocktopher Lady' Mini* — Low-petaled, orange-pink striped blooms. Mild fragrance.

'Kiss 'n' Tell', Min

'Kiss the Bride', Min

'Lady in Red', Min

'Laura's Laughter', Min

'Little White Lies', Min

'Lovers Only', Min

'Ladies' View' Mini — An old-fashioned bloom bearing quilled petals in a delicate shade of apricot.

'Lady Be Good' Mini** — Medium pink blooms having a mild fragrance. Named for the Gershwin musical.

'Lady in Red' Mini — Scarlet red blooms with a slight silver reverse. Also a good seed provider for the breeder.

'Laura's Laughter' Mini — Named for our eldest granddaughter. A low-growing plant with dusky pink blooms and a silver reverse. Laura was in the greenhouse with me one day when we decided that this little rose should be named for her. She burst out with delighted laughter, hence the name.

'Little Breeze' Mini — A short plant with strongly scented orange blend flowers. One of my earliest roses, unfortunately lost in the mists of time.

'Little White Lies' Mini — Single white blooms on a good shrub, and, picking up what someone said on the Internet, "a damn good rose."

'Looks Like Fun' Mini — Heavily mottled, pastel pink stripes across a white background. Low-growing plant with a sprawling habit.

'Lovers Only' Mini — Highly pointed buds of Chinese red reversed in straw-yellow, opens to form classic hybrid tea blooms.

'Margaret Telfer' Mini* — Large white blooms with a mild fragrance.

'Mary 'n' John' MinFl — Blooms are medium yellow with an occasional pink touch to the petals. Well shaped in the hybrid tea manner; flowers are generally carried in groups of three, occasionally one to a stem. Soft fragrance; few prickles.

'Mary Toomey' Mini* — Yellow blend blooms.

'Misty Eyed' MinFl — Blooms are white with a greyish tint—like a tear drop!

'Mouse' Mini* — Low-petaled flowers of medium pink with yellow at the base; borne in small clusters with a slight fragrance.

'Near You' Cl. Mini — Light yellow, high-centered blooms of about 2 inches cover this 5-foot climber.

'Misty Eyed', MiniFl

'Portland Dawn' Mini — Spring brings light pink, and the arrival of autumn is signaled by almost orange hues. Spicy perfume.

'Rich and Rare' Mini* — Red blend blooms with a modest fragrance.

'Portland Dawn', Min

'Rosey Lou' Mini — Blooms with a blend of deep and medium pinks.

'San Francisco Sunset' Mini — Burnt-orange, well-shaped blooms on an enthusiastic grower.

'Someday Soon' Mini — Ovoid-shaped, light yellow buds uncurl to form lemon colored, high-centered blooms. Like a number of my yellow roses this often produces a white bloom, but don't be distracted as the change does not last!

'Rosey Lou', Min

'Stolen Moment' Cl Mini — Ah! My real favorite of them all. Deep mauve blooms, burnished with a reddish blush as they age. The plant reaches 6 feet in height and blooms profusely.

'Street Wise' Mini — Hybridized by our youngest son Ronan. A bright rainbow of orange and pink shadings. Disease resistance is said to be phenomenal.

'Stolen Moment', Cl Min

'SWALK' Cl Mini — Lovely red with silver-backed blooms that are fragrant and well shaped, on a miniature climber to 6 feet. The name comes from a time when, as tender youths, we would put this on the back of an envelope "Sealed With A Loving Kiss."

'Swansong' Mini — After 'Admirable', this is my most fragrant

'Fair Eva', Min

'SWALK', Cl Min

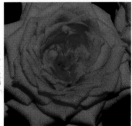

'Swansong', Min

'Tantalizing Mary', MinFl

'Tatooed Lady', Min

'The Magic Man', Min

rose, with fragrance that will fill a room with its spicy bouquet. Blooms again have that uncertainty between white and a soft shading of apricot. I found this one day among my seedlings when I seemed to be very ill and thought that this was my "swansong." Well, the rose took the name — and I didn't take the hint!

'Tantalizing Mary' MinFl — Yellow blend, very fragrant, full, mostly one-to-a-stem blooms age to apricot centers on an upright and bushy plant. The lady for whom this was named, Mary Pullen, had a tantalizing time as she waited to see which rose I selected for her.

'Tattooed Lady' Mini — Red blooms mottled and striped with yellow. Mild fragrance.

'The Magic Man' Mini — A good striped bloom in pink and yellow. Named because some of my grandchildren called me this when I produced goodies when they visited!

'Toffee' (Keeva) Mini — Burnt orange, decorative blooms, borne singly on long, stiff stems. As the blooms age, the color deepens for a very attractive effect.

'True Vintage' Mini — Medium red blooms with a color tending toward fuchsia, with a moderate, fruity fragrance. Compact plant.

'Velvet Cloak' Mini — Dark, velvety red petals and prominent yellow stamens.

'Wishful Thinking' Mini — Bright, carmine red petals reversed in yellow with a good fragrance.

'Wit's End' Mini — Shimmering orange petals with a reverse of straw yellow. Very glossy foliage. Erma Bombeck was the writer of a family column under this name and so it seemed an appropriate name for the only rose I had that was a success in its collection.

'You 'n' Me' Mini — This was my very first rose to be introduced, and has been previously described in this chapter.

As well as these miniature or Mini-Flora varieties, I have also had a number of large roses introduced, mainly by Ashdown Roses. These include:

'Wit's End', Min

'Alluring' HT — Bright pink flowers finish with red outer petals. High-centered blooms with moderate fragrance on an upright plant.

'Ava Rose' Fl — A 'Playboy' seedling named by California rosarian Alice Flores in her granddaughter's honor. Creamy, large flowers; flat, distinctive and welcoming.

'Alluring', HT

'Big Jim Larkin' HT — A fragrant hand painted rose of red with a distinctive silver reverse. Blooms tend to hang their heads. The grandson of this famous Irish politician came to my garden one day, saw this rose, and asked if it could be named for his grandfather.

'Big Jim Larkin', HT

'Bloomsday' Fl — Orange blend floribunda with blooms aging to a distinctive dark brown. This rose first came into bloom in my garden on June 16, the day celebrated in Ireland that coincides with the part of the novel of the same name in James Joyce's *Ulysses*. I was not feeling the best of form on that morning and one daughter suggested that I had climbed out of the bed on the wrong side — which was how Joyce depicted Mr. Bloom. So the rose just had to be 'Bloomsday'.

'Buttermilk Sky', Fl

'Buttermilk Sky' Fl — Creamy, well shaped blooms with a strong fragrance, forming in large clusters that dislike the rain!

Cancan Swirl Fl — Renamed 'Christine Marina'.

'Caroline Louise' HT — Very large, very fragrant apricot blend blooms.

'Celeb' Sh — Massed heads of apricot-pink in the old-fashioned style.

'Wishful Thinking', Min

'Christine Marina' Fl — A mauve rose, medium in size with full blooms of moderate fragrance. Flowers carried in good

'Caroline Louise', HT

'Celeb', S

'Christina Marina', F

'Gentle Annie', F

'Girl Friday', F

clusters, and are distinguished by open flat blooms with a suggestion of lighter edges.

'Colin's Fubar' HT — Large, pink, well-shaped blooms with a strong fragrance.

'Dr. John' HT — Mauve pink blooms.

'Eustacia' FL — Hand painted floribunda in shades of pink.

'Gentle Annie' Fl — Large, low-petaled, fuchsia/mauve blooms with a light aroma.

'Gerry Hughes' HT — Large, cream-to-pink blooms.

'Girl Friday' Fl — Yellowish blooms that age to a light tan.

'Gossamer Wings' Sh — Silvery pink, low-petalled blooms on a moderate sized plant of up to 5 feet.

'Height of Fashion' Fl — Apricot-pink blooms forming in small clusters; little to no fragrance.

'Highland's Rose' Fl — Medium pink blossoms; slight fragrance.

'Kilkea Castle' Sh — Fragrant, pink-blend blooms on a medium-sized bush. This was once a famous castle in Ireland, but is now a hotel.

'Margaret McDowell' HT — Medium red, mildly fragrant blooms on a low-growing plant.

'Martin Martin' HT — Large, high-centered blooms of white with a red edge. The man for whom this was named was a great exhibitor and writer on roses from California.

'Molly Bloom' HT — Large, pink blooms. Named for the heroine of the James Joyce novel *Ulysses*.

'Murphy's Law' HT — Very large, very fragrant pink blooms;

an offspring of 'Fragrant Cloud'.

'Murphy's Law', HT

'My Wild Irish Rose' Sh — A shrub/climber up to 7 feet with big heads of lovely, single, pink and white blooms.

'Oonagh' HT — Medium red flowers with a mild fragrance. Named for our second daughter. I have always said the boys in the family get a football while the girls get a rose. I know who gets the best deal!

'My Wild Irish Rose', S

'Sally Mac' Fl — Named for my wife. A lovely confection of orange, pink and apricot blooms with a strong fragrance.

'Siobhan' Fl — Red blooms, yellow reverse, mild fragrance. Named for our eldest daughter, who reluctantly agreed to my request that she pick a seedling. One day, under duress, she "accepted" this one. She could not have picked a better one, even though she was rushing off to a date.

'Sally Mac', F

'Spitfire Paddy' HT — Named in honor of an air ace of World War II. Large orange, pink and yellow blooms.

'Warm Heart' Sh — Shrub/short climber to about 8 feet. Orange blend blooms.

'Siobhan', F

* *Never introduced into commerce* Many of my roses have been named for people: family, friends, neighbors, that sort of thing. Others have been given names that simply strike my mind. Often, when someone said they liked a particular rose, I would give it to them; however, that was occasionally the only plant I had of that variety. It would then stay in their garden and never be introduced. However, I did keep records, and registered nearly all my roses because I thought that was important. This is why you will find names like 'Rich and Rare' or 'Margaret Telfer' in sources such as *Modern Roses* or www.HelpMeFind.com when, in fact, the roses themselves never made it to the market, either in Europe or the United States.

** These varieties were lost, at least to me, with the dispersal of plants at Justice Miniature Roses following the death of the owner.

'Spitfire Paddy', HT

'True Vintage', Min

Chapter 13
Selected List

*When writing this selected list, I thought of the words of Dean Hole, a rose lover, author and Dean of Rochester Cathedral in England a century and a quarter ago, when he wrote about "a delicious perplexity, an ecstasy of amazement, an embarrassment of riches...a sweet uncertainty" when faced with having to make a similar selection. As I made it, I realized that there are many roses here that are not officially classified as Mini-Floras, but as they **could** all fall into this category, I have included them, and for the moment I will settle for this "delicious perplexity."*

'Alexa' MinFl, Mitchie Moe. Lightly fragrant, beautiful deep pink blooms that become a lighter shade of pink as the petals unfurl. Blooms have a very high center and are exhibition quality, but exhibitors will want to cut them tight.

'Always A Lady' Mini, Dee Bennett. Lavender blooms with perfect show form and a soft, sweet fragrance. Long-stemmed blooms are usually borne one to a stem. A great rose for a container or for garden display in rich lavender.

'Amber Flash' MinFl, J. Benjamin Williams. Perfectly formed buds blossom into gracefully shaped blooms in an eye-opening yellow-orange blend. Forces well and performs well outdoors. Height to 20 inches. A rose that has been available for 20 years and is consistently used by florists and arrangers for its great bloom shape.

'Amy Grant' MinFl, Robbie Tucker. Very light pink flowers with hybrid tea form. Excellent for garden or container, and also as a cut flower.

'Astra' Mini, J. Benjamin Williams. A unique low-growing plant that bears clusters of up to a dozen pink, dogwood-like blossoms. Will grow to 12 inches high with a breadth of 18 inches.

'Autumn Splendor' MinFl, Michael C. Williams. Originally registered as a miniature, it has been changed to a Mini-Flora.

'Amy Grant', MinFl

'Always a Lady', Min

'Amber Flash', MinFl

Bright orange blooms with golden yellow centers and good exhibition form. The bushes grow quite large with lots of good blooms.

'Baby Love' Mini, Len Scrivens. Sold worldwide as the disease free, no-spray rose. It can get little marks on the foliage, but scientists say that these are a result of the plant fighting off blackspot! A bushy space filler with single yellow flowers and good, distinctive fragrance. In recent times it has fallen afoul of more persistent blackspot in some areas.

'Bella Via' MinFl, Herb Zipper. Excellent rose for exhibition. Non-fading blooms with excellent substance, white with a hint of light yellow, borne on straight stems with high-centered form.

'Bellissima' MinFl, Zipper. Orange red blooms, darker along the edges, exhibition form, double, borne one to a stem, no fragrance. Upright growth with good vigor.

'Cachet' MinFl, Tucker. A pure white rose that was partially responsible for the new Mini-Flora category. Originally registered as a miniature, the bloom was always considered too large for the group. But for all that, it was still able to make the top 15 of mini show roses in the United States. 'Cachet' means a mark of distinction, a name certainly merited by its long-lasting, high-centered, large, white blooms that are an exhibitor's delight, as well as an excellent cut flower.

'Carrot Top' (formerly Panache) Mini, Poulsens. Bright orange that does not fade; good healthy foliage on a bushy plant. Use as a mass planting for the full effect of the eye-catching blooms.

'Celebration 2000' Shrub, Colin Horner. Bright, unfading, yellow blooms with a reverse slightly lighter. Semi-double blooms produced in large clusters. There is some fragrance. The foliage is strikingly glossy, while the new growth has reddish stems. Awarded a Trial Grounds Certificate in the 1997 Royal National Rose Society Trials.

'Checkmate' MinFl, Tucker. The breeder calls this a "chameleon" as its bright red buds open to orange-pink. When fully open the flowers show a creamy white center. Exhibition type blooms.

'Baby Love', Min

'Cougar' MinFl, Moe. Upright, vigorous growing bush with exhibition-form blooms that are fragrant, with a medium red on the upper petal surfaces and a light pink reverse. Named by the breeder for the colors that reminded her of those of Washington State University and their mascot—the cougar.

'Cream Puff' MinFl, Bennett. Semi-double blooms in soft cream with a delicate blush of pink; most beautiful when fully open.

'Dilly Dilly' MinFl, Bennett. A rich lavender bloom color, with hybrid tea form and good fragrance.

'Cachet', MinFl

'Dolly Dot' MinFl Jackson & Perkins. Deep yellow blooms. The giant of the rose industry released this pretty rose.

'Dolores Marie' MinFl, Tucker. Highly fragrant blooms that are mauve with darker mauve edges. Exhibition form at the half to three-quarters open stage, but then takes on the look of an old garden rose when fully open, with a petal count of 40 plus. The rose got its name when a man in the Nashville area purchased it as an anniversary present for his wife.

'Donna Jean' Fl, Kay and Pete Taylor. Lavender, semi-double blooms opening to show a white eye; dark green foliage on a medium-sized plant.

'Carrot Top', Min

'Dr. John Dickman' MinFl, Dennis Bridges. Lovely, well-formed blooms of deep purple, edged with red. A tall plant, named for the American Rose Society's "Q & A" columnist.

'Ferrin' MinFl, Tucker. A very consistent winner in shows. Medium pink-coral blooms with pinpoint centers. Usually produces one bloom to a stem, but can also develop sprays. A beautiful rose at all stages of bloom and a great cut flower.

'Ferrin', MinFl

'Flora Bama' Mini, Taylors. Long stems with red blooms opening to a white center; slightly spreading plant with dark green foliage.

'Checkmate', MinFl

'Cream Puff', MinFl

'Dolores Marie', MinFl

'Dr. John Dickman', MinFl

'Free As Air' Mini, Bernhard Mehring. One of those "odd" colored roses that always attracts attention. This one is orange-red with brownish-tan, a unique coloring. Bushy and free flowering, it was named to commemorate the British Asthma Campaign.

'Gail' MinFl, Bennett. Golden yellow flowers that change to orange and finally red. Nicely formed blooms make it good for exhibitors. Like many other roses in this category, 'Gail' was first registered as a mini, then as a Mini-Flora. (note: Sue O'Brien, Dee Bennett's daughter, says: "On request from various people this rose has been reclassified twice. I refuse to move it again, no matter who begs me to change it.").

'Georgia Belle' MinFl, Taylors. Beautiful peach/coral blooms with good form; long stems and dark green foliage on a vigorous plant with abundant blooms.

'Gold Symphonie' Mini, Meilland. Strong, compact, healthy bush that carries delightful yellow blooms.

'Golden Fox' MinFl, Chris Warner. Deep yellow blooms. Very well received in Europe and Australia, where it has been highly placed in numerous rose trials. Also known as Golden Handshake in the United Kingdom and Australia.

"Hit" Roses, Poulsen. A wide range of patio style roses bred by Poulsens of Denmark. The varieties are compact and designed for the gift plant markets; each pot usually contains about four rooted cuttings that are easily adapted to garden or increased pot use. The series begins with 'Absolute Hit' (orange-red) and carries the "Hit" name through a collection of just about every color. *All are classified as miniatures.*

'Honky Tonk' Mini, Taylors. Bright red blooms with a white reverse. Hybrid tea form, opens quickly; dark green foliage on a medium-sized showy plant

Kordana Series, W. Kordes' Söhne of Germany is the largest and perhaps one of the most complete rose hybridizing companies in the world, producing a whole range of roses, from miniatures right through to climbers and all types of large roses. Since 1990, Kordes has conducted extensive hybridization of miniatures for the potted floral trade. Called Kordana roses, their increasing popularity is due to an exciting range of colors, large hybrid tea-shaped flowers, healthy, dark green foliage and excellent keeping characteristics. Although these varieties have been produced for growing indoors, most are suitable for outdoor containers, patio pots and balcony boxes, as well as later planting in the open soil in gardens.

'Free as Air', Min

Kordana roses are generally produced by specialist growers in efficient, modern glasshouses that afford year-round flowering. Most typically, flowering Kordana plants are available from retail nurseries, home centers and supermarket florists. The Kordana collection consists of more than 80 varieties, in a wide range of colors, many of which are fine exhibition types. Most of the varieties are patented. Although registration to date of has been limited in the United States, a number of the Kordana varieties have won awards in European rose competitions, among them 'Vanilla' and 'Evita Kordana'. Varieties produced specifically by W. Kordes Söhne for outdoor use include 'Bordeaux Kordana', 'Esmeralda Kordana', 'Orange Kordana', 'Sunbeam Kordana' and 'Vanilla Kordana'.

'Gail', MinFl

'Gold Symphonie', Min

'Lady E'owyn' (pronounced A-o-when) MinFl, Tucker. Red-blend blooms with long straight stems. Definitely one for the exhibitor. The blooms have a very high petal count, are extremely long lasting and show the best color when grown in full sunlight. Here is a tip from the hybridizer: "While the form is extremely long-lasting it should be cut at about a quarter open stage and brought indoors. Continue to groom a little at a time over the next 24 hours and then refrigerate." Not too many breeders give this positive advice about their blooms. 'Lady E'owyn' was named in honor of the heroine of J.R.R. Tolkien's *The Lord of the Rings*.

'Lazy Daze' Mini, Taylors. Lavender blooms with a darker reverse; heavily petaled, sometimes reminiscent of an old garden rose. Dark green foliage on a medium-sized plant.

'Absolute Hit', Min

'Bordeaux Kordana', Min

'Esmerelda Kordana', Min

'Orange Kordana', Min

'Lady E' owyn', MinFl

'Lois' Mini, Bennett. Blooms of pinkish lavender on a fast-growing bush; lots of long-stemmed, hybrid tea-type blooms in a shade of mauve, but with hints of pink. Usually borne one-to-a-stem, the flowers may also come in small sprays.

'Love Note' MinFl, Zipper. Deep pink to light red blooms lightening to cream at the base, with a reverse of deep pink; 35 petals, exhibition form, slight fragrance, bushy and tall growth. A good garden rose, and very good for exhibition. In cool weather the colors intensify.

'**Madeline Spezzano'** MinFl, Bennett. Perhaps one of the best of the late Dee Bennett's Mini-Floras. It is rich pink with excellent, long-lasting form. Heavily petaled; the blooms take days to open.

"Meillandina" series, Meilland. An early series of small roses produced by Meilland in France, covering most colors and types for both garden and container growing. *All are classified as miniatures.*

'Money For Nothing' Mini, Taylors. Creamy apricot blooms with a darker base. It has excellent hybrid tea form and a soft fragrance, long stems with medium green foliage on an upright plant. "Creating a rose with these qualities is a nice reward for such an enjoyable effort" says Kay Taylor. Named after the hit song by Dire Straits.

'Night Music' MinFl, Zipper. Deep pink (light red) large blooms borne singly and in sprays, exhibition form, nice fragrance. A good garden variety, vigorous, winter hardy.

'Old Fashioned Girl' Mini, Bennett. This seedling of 'Sombreuil' starts out looking like a hybrid tea, but opens with a form more similar to its old garden rose parent. The white blooms have a wonderful fragrance.

'Overnight Scentsation' MinFl, Saville. The rose that was carried in a rocket to outer space in order to study the effects of perfume under those conditions. It carries largish flowers in a deep pink color that will make an exhibition bloom when caught early.

Palace Series, Poulsens. A further group of small roses produced by the Danish firm. These are particularly effective as compact plants carrying clusters of blooms that open to what they call a "tudor patio," in other words an old-fashioned style bloom on a modern low-growing bush. The series now runs to some 40 varieties, and includes 'Crystal Palace' (creamy peach), 'Grand Palace' (deep red) and 'Joey's Palace' (amber orange). While growing on their own roots in a container, the plants stay quite small, but in the open garden they can take on the suggestion of a shrub or floribunda. *Some are classified as miniatures, some as Mini-Floras and some as shrubs.*

'Lois', Min

'Patio Dance', 'Patio Gold', 'Patio Jewel', 'Patio Pearl', 'Patio Ribbon', 'Patio Snow' MinFl, J.B. Williams. These form part of the large number of Mini-Flora roses introduced by the man who is credited with the introduction of the whole group, J. Benjamin Williams of Silver Spring, MD.

'Patriot's Dream' MinFl, Michael C. Williams. High-centered blooms produced on long, straight stems. Ruby red with white at the base of the petals and a white reverse. A vigorous grower.

'Madeline Spezzano', MinFl

'Percussion' Fl, Zipper. Dark red with a touch of yellow at the base, white brushed with red reverse. Exhibition form, 25 petals, moderate sweet fragrance, borne singly and in small sprays of three to five blooms, upright bushy growth.

'Playmate' Fl, Horner. Orange/apricot blend with a lighter orange reverse. Good fragrance in the semi-double blooms, which are produced in large clusters on a very free-flowering plant. The foliage is small, glossy and medium green in color, and the habit is bushy. The parentage is 'Baby Love' x 'Lolita' (LitaKOR). Awarded a Certificate of Merit in the Royal National Rose Society Trials and a Gold Medal in the Dublin Trials.

'Old Fashioned Girl', Min

'Prom Night' MinFl, Zipper. Creamy yellow-to-pink shadings, with deep pink flushing at the petal edges, very double, slight fragrance, foliage large, medium green matte. Blooms hold very well. According to the hybridizer, "Three blooms, and you have a large corsage, which is the rationale for the name."

'Overnight Scentsation', MinFl

'Crystal Palace', Fl

'Joey's Palace', S

'Patriot's Dream', MinFl

'Quiet Time', MinFl

'Pzazz Hit' MinFl, Poulsens. "Style, striped and stinky" are what distinguishes this 1996 patio from the Danish firm. Double flowers are a combination of pink and cerise, softening as the flower ages.

'Quiet Time' MinFl, Bennett. Tiny Petals Nursery stopped selling this rose many years ago; but some folks are still growing and even showing it. The soft lavender blooms have a slightly tan center and hybrid tea form.

'Raspberry Ice' MinFl, Zipper. White brushed with red, deeper red at petal edge, large, double, 40 petals, exhibition blooms borne singly or in sprays of three.

'Rita Applegate' MinFl, Bennett. Soft honey/gold blooms with beautiful show form.

'Riverdance' Mini, David Kenny. A deep pink patio rose that produces a huge number of fragrant flowers over a long period, usually from early summer to the advent of the first severe frosts of winter. It has a rounded, bushy habit with very good resistance to disease. This rose won the top award in the patio/mini/climber section at the Dublin International Rose Trials and a Certificate of Merit in Belfast. Jan Spek Rozen released it in Europe in 2002.

'Roxie' MinFl, Tucker. Another rose that has been held back for the Mini-Flora class. Pinpoint centers that last for many days. In most cases, the bloom never opens beyond exhibition stage. Color is a solid orange and the petals "snap" into place with the slightest coaxing. The foliage is dark green and very glossy. The plant produces a rounded bush and grows to 3 feet.

'Ruffian' MinFl, David Clemons. Salmon blooms with pinpoint centers make it an ideal exhibitor's rose, but because it has only about 17 petals, it must be caught quickly! Opens to a very attractive bloom.

'Shine On' Mini, Colin Dickson. Endorsed as a Breeder's Award winner in the United Kingdom in 1994, the full flowers are a pink-orange blend. A reliable producer of blooms over a long period.

'Silverhill' Mini, Taylors. Pinkish/mauve blooms with a lighter reverse appearing almost silver. High, pointed bloom form, long straight stems and dark green foliage on an upright plant. Nice for exhibiting, cut blooms and the garden.

'Something For Judy' MinFl, Bennett. Semi-double blooms in soft cream to gold that blush salmon pink to red in the sun.

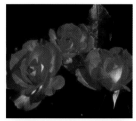

'Raspberry Ice', MinFl

'Spring's A Comin'' MinFl, Whit Wells. Pink blend blooms on a very floriferous, vigorous bush.

'Stardance' MinFl, J. B. Williams. A real Mini-Flora star, 'Stardance' blooms are an elegant white accented by a burst of yellow in the center. A vigorous grower, it will easily reach 24 inches in height.

'Rita Applegate', MinFl

'Starship' MinFl, Bridges. Exhibition style blooms of deep golden yellow with a coral blush.

Sunblaze Series, Meilland. A long running and very successful series of roses that are ideal for gardens or containers. The series includes such first class varieties as 'Sunny Sunblaze' (buff), 'Classic Sunblaze' (rich, vibrant pink), 'Lady Sunblaze' (soft pink), 'Magic Sunblaze' (creamy white edged in tones ranging from pink to scarlet) and 'Orange Sunblaze' (brilliant orange flowers even in the most intense heat). *All are classified as miniatures.*

'Roxie', MinFl

'Sweet Arlene' MinFl, Bennett. Very pale lavender blooms with hybrid form and incredible fragrance.

'Sweet Dream' Fl, Fryer. Cupped blooms with striking form and deep apricot flowers. A vigorous grower and a good producer of blooms over a long period.

'Orange Sunblaze', Min

'Sweet Magic' Mini, Pat Dickson. From the firm in Northern Ireland with a great track record in producing roses of patio size. Orange and gold perfumed blooms.

'Tear Drop' Mini, Pat Dickson. Brilliantly white blooms with prominent yellow stamens. This variety has a great record for

'Shine On', Min

'Something for Judy', MinFl

'Stardance', MinFl

'Starship', MinFl

'Sweet Magic', Min

'Tear Drop', Min

surviving heavy rain.

'Tennessee Sunrise' MinFl, Whit Wells. Long lasting, high-centered blooms of eye-catching deep orange-yellow with red edge. Robust bush.

'Tiffany Lite' MinFl, Diann Giles. A sport of 'Tiffany Lynn', one of the early Mini-Floras. Blooms are ivory in color and have excellent high-centered exhibition form. The petals have very good substance.

'Violet Mist' MinFl, Bennett. Perfectly formed blooms in soft lavender abound on a big plant. This rose makes a great garden display and is good for exhibition.

'War Dance' (Fiesta) Fl, Sam McGredy. A patio-type rose that will prove a novelty anywhere with its hand-painted, freely produced blooms that are scarlet with a silvery white margin and a creamy white reverse. Another McGredy rose not generally accepted as a Mini-Flora but which fits into the category due to its garden growth is 'Regensberg', also hand-painted and a beautiful addition to any garden. There is also a sport of 'Regensberg' called 'Greenall's Glory', a much lighter-toned bloom, found in the United Kingdom by Gordon Kirkham.

'What A Peach' S, Warner. Delicious peachy color on a plant called a "shrublet" by Weeks Roses in the United States. This lovely, bushy plant is a patio everywhere else and certainly fits into the Mini-Flora scheme of things.

'White Roadrunner' Hybrid Rugosa, Uhl. A very unusual rose, offered by Kordes of Germany as the first rugosa in the patio/Mini-Flora grouping.

'Yantai' MinFl, Bennett. The flowers are cream to soft yellow with a deeper yellow center. In warmer weather, the blooms will have a delicate blush of pink. The heavily petaled flowers last for weeks on the bush or as cut bouquets.

'Foolish Pleasure', MinFl

'Sunny Sunblaze', Min

Chapter 14
The Future?

It doesn't need a rose of a certain era to turn misery into happiness; for that single thing I am grateful to the rose. It means that I can love all roses: old or new, past, present or future.

Give it five years at the most, and I believe that the Mini-Flora rose will be one of the main sellers in the rose world. To most people it is already an overnight sensation, but like most overnight sensations it has taken 30 years to be acknowledged. It was time well spent.

One leading California rose breeder, nurseryman and writer, Kim Rupert, put it succinctly when he said: "Mini-Floras are going to be more prevalent as long as gardens continue to downsize, and balconies become more the norm. As hybrid teas and floribundas get larger and spaces become smaller, the demand for smaller plants with larger blooms increases. I have many people regularly inquiring about roses that will do well in pots and fit well on their balcony or deck gardens. These smaller plants with showier flowers tend to be more of what they're looking for."

Today, as you will have seen in this short book, the Mini-Flora is in fact well on its way to success. The dedication of a small number of people have put it on its pedestal and encouraged others to acknowledge it along the way. At first it was disparaged as not being a rose that would have a place in our gardens. Now no matter where you look in the hybridizing houses of today, small or large, you will find whole benches of Mini-Flora seedlings all looking for a place among the big roses.

An enormous amount of perseverance from people like J. Benjamin Williams has spurred a whole industry to back his belief in this rose, and huge amounts of money, time and effort have been put into research that is paying off in a big way.

Not only in America ,but throughout the world, everyone seems to be following the same path with roses of style and promise, mainly of the MiniFlora type. The main hope is that these new roses will introduce better, longer-lasting flowers than the miniatures and more disease resistance than the bigger forms

'Yantai', MinFl

'Tiffany Lite', MinFl

'Violet Mist', MinFl

of the rose.

In New Zealand, Australia, South Africa and Britain, the Mini-Flora is there, often lurking under another name—Sunspot, fairytale, patio, Sunblaze, Kordana, Palace or hobbit roses. But what's in a name? They are all aimed at producing the same sort of plant: bushy, bountiful and beautiful.

Frank Benardella, a leading American hybridizer who was not initially in favor of the classification being granted to the Mini-Flora, has since told me: "I wish you could see the bloom on some of the larger miniatures in the greenhouse now that will fit into the MiniFlora class. The blooms have absolutely perfect exhibition style. I am really excited about them. And to think that for the last five years I have been trying to breed everything smaller. How wrong was I?"

In Europe, Colin Dickson, of the famous Northern Ireland hybridizing family, says he believes that there is a great future for the Mini-Flora rose: "Most of the European patio roses grow too tall to be considered Mini-Flora but they are on the right track. They will lead us to more and better roses in these categories."

Bernhard F. Mehring, rose breeder and agent, is convinced of the rosy future for containerized roses, not only in England, where he lives, but on a far wider scale. He realizes that this market is dominated by impulse purchasing, which means that an attractive plant in flower will make an impact with purchasers quicker than the traditional hybrid teas and floribundas, which will lose out because they generally produce fewer blooms. The miniature, too, is losing out because it cannot stand up to the harsh treatment received at today's retail centers. So the world is opening up for the Mini-Flora.

Top breeders in the United States are setting out their stalls with many of these new varieties, aiming at selling them directly to the public through the Internet. This is another area that will expand as more and more hybridizers establish their own websites.

All of which is just one more indication that what is now a mere stream of new varieties will soon become a flood.

The larger-than-miniature bloom on a small bush will change every gardener's life. There will be deviations in growth that will become obvious; in some places such as California and Florida, many of the varieties may grow taller than expected, but the beauty and adaptability of the Mini-Flora will always be present. While the initial impetus was for one-to-a-stem double blooms with a high-pointed center, this is already changing to incorporate not only spray blooms in a floribunda style, but even single roses. The colors are all there too, and very fragrant varieties are being welcomed. There will be many other variations on the theme. Soon there will be recognition of short climbers (there are many already available, such as 'SWALK') while the German firm of Kordes has flagged other possibilities with their rugosa Mini-Flora, 'White Roadrunner', which could capture a place with the ruggedness of its rugosa breeding.

The future is in the past, and I regard the Mini-Flora as a visitor bringing me greetings and memories of thousands of roses from years gone by. It won't be a flickering visit; the Mini-Flora is very much here to stay. It will take its place in the wonderful pantheon of the world's great roses.

Sean McCann

'Liberty Bell', MinFl

'Tiffany Lynn', MinFl

'Will-o'-the-Wisp', MinFl

Appendix A

J. Benjamin Williams Mini-Flora Rose National Trophy
Spring & Fall National Conventions

Year	Name	City/State	Awarded at	Roses
2006 Spring	Harold & Jean Baker	Lakeland, FL	Seattle, WA	'Butter Cream' 'Cachet' 'Foolish Pleasure' 'Louisville Lady' 'Solar Flair'
2005 Fall	Harold & Jean Baker	Lakeland,FL	Memphis, TN	'Butter Cream' 'Cachet' 'Lady E'owyn' 'Louisville Lady' 'Memphis King'
2005 Spring	Harold & Jean Baker	Lakeland,FL	Shreveport, LA	'Butter Cream' 'Cachet' 'Camden' 'Charismatic' 'Class of '73' 'Conundrum' 'Dr John Dickman' 'Louisville Lady' 'Solar Flair' 'Tiffany Lynn'
2004 Fall	Sandy & Bob Lundberg	Bluffton, SC	Tulsa, OK	'Butter Cream' 'Cachet' 'Foolish Pleasure' 'Lady E'owyn' 'Peter Cottontail'
2004 Spring	Dr. & Mrs. Satish Prabhu	Columbia, SC	San Diego, CA	'Aliena' 'Bella Via' 'Cachet' 'Conundrum' 'Tiffany Lynn'
2003 Fall	Dr. & Mrs. Satish Prabhu	Columbia, SC	Washington DC	'Bella Via' 'Cachet' 'Conundrum' 'Lady E'owyn' 'Tiffany Lynn'
2003 Spring	Sandy & Bob Lundberg	Bluffton, SC	New Orleans, LA	'Bella Via' 'Cachet' 'Ruffian' 'Tiffany Lite' 'Tiffany Lynn'

Year	Name	City/State	Awarded at	Roses
2002 Fall	Dr. & Mrs. Satish Prabhu	Columbia, SC	Philadelphia, PA	'Amy Grant' 'Bella Via' 'Ferrin' 'Lady E'owyn' 'Tiffany Lynn'
2001 Fall	Dr. & Mrs. Satish Prabhu	Columbia, SC	Cleveland, OH	'Amy Grant' 'Bella Via' 'Cachet' 'Ferrin' 'Tiffany Lynn'
2000 Fall	Sandy & Bob Lundberg	Bluffton, SC	Atlanta, GA	'Autumn Splendor' 'Bella Via' 'Patriot's Dream' 'Tiffany Lynn' 'Violet Mist'

Mini-Flora Queen of Show

Year	Name	City/State	Awarded at	Rose
2006	Linda Clark	San Diego, CA	Spring Nat'l@ Seattle, WA	'Camden'
2005	Tammy Boswell	Bartlett, TN	Fall Nat'l@ Memphis, TN	Louisville Lady'
2005	Sandy & Bob Lundberg	Bluffton, SC	Mini Conference@ Indianapolis, IN	'Peter Cottontail'
2005	Barbara Olive	Bartlett, TN	Spring Nat'l@ Shreveport, LA	'Tiffany Lynn'
2003	Paul & Charlotte Blankenship	North Augusta, SC	Mini Conference@ Charleston, SC	'Tiffany Lynn'

Appendix B
Judging Mini-Flora Specimens

DEFINITION
The Mini-Flora classification is a new American term given to the ARS for use by hybridizer J. Benjamin Williams. The Mini-Flora class was developed for cultivars in which bloom and bush size grow too large to be classed as miniatures. The class shows many characteristics of the hybrid teas in both form and a tendency to bloom as a one-bloom-per-stem specimen. At the national level the Mini-Flora is ineligible to compete for the miniature Queen or Court. The abbreviation for the class is MinFl.

DISBUDDING
Mini-Flora rose specimens may be shown as one-bloom-per stem or sprays. The one-bloom-per stem entries must be shown disbudded. All the penalty and disqualification rules that apply to hybrid tea specimens also apply to the Mini-Flora class.

STEM-ON-STEM
A stem-on-stem on a Mini-Flora specimen is a disqualification.

POINT SCORING
```
FORM ..................................................... 25
COLOR ............................................ 20
SUBSTANCE ................................ 15
STEM AND FOLIAGE ...................................... 20
BALANCE AND PROPORTION ...................... 10
SIZE ................................................. 10
TOTAL ............................................. 100
```

The same point values allotted to the six prime elements of judging for hybrid teas, grandifloras, floribundas and miniatures are also applied to Mini-Floras. The judge must constantly remember that the values allotted to the six prime elements are maximum values for absolute perfection. Leeway must be allowed for that ever-present possibility of encountering a better specimen of that variety.

Judging One-Bloom-per-Stem Mini-Floras
Detailed Application of the Six Prime Elements of Judging

FORM

As with the hybrid tea and grandiflora, the Mini-Flora bloom can represent both the classic hybrid tea form as well as decorative form. The classic hybrid tea form displays a high pointed center, with petals unfurling from the point in a symmetrical spiral to the outer row of petals that ideally, but not always, depending upon the variety, lay along a horizontal plane. The ideal degree of openness of the blooms is the same as that for hybrid teas, that is, two-thirds to three-fourths open or with four to five rows of petals unfurling between the high center and the outer petals. Split, confused, balled or snub-nosed centers and recurved petals (petals that fold in and do not open to follow the natural spiral) are penalized according to the degree that these defects detract from the beauty of the bloom. Fewer-petaled Mini-Floras that still maintain a high pointed center as they open should be one-third to one-half open, that is, with three or four rows of petals symmetrically unfurling. When viewed in profile, the high-pointed center and symmetry of the bloom should be apparent. When viewed from above, the petal edges should lay within an imaginary circle circumscribing the perimeter of the bloom. In general, the Form element follows exactly that of the hybrid tea on a reduced-size scale.

COLOR

The same 18 color classes apply to the Mini-Flora class. The color should be bright, clear, blemish-free and typical of the variety. The green and white streaks often found in white and red roses, respectively, are color faults and should be penalized according to the degree of distraction. However, color-striping characteristic of some varieties is not a fault, but the striping should be uniformly distributed throughout the petalage to preserve color symmetry. The "blueing" of certain varieties, namely, the reds, is often the result of refrigeration and is a detraction from the normal color of the rose and, hence, should be penalized.

SUBSTANCE

Petal and foliage crispness is an indication of healthy substance.

STEM AND FOLIAGE

Stem and foliage constitute the physical and visual support of the specimen. The stem should be straight, bearing a bloom that is erect and not drooping. The prickles should be intact above the rim of the container. The foliage should be evenly distributed along the stem and provide a circular and symmetrical background of green for the bloom when it is viewed from above.

Skillful trimming of the foliage is permitted and is not penalized unless it constitutes a distraction. Both stem and foliage should be free from insect or disease damage and should be clean, subject to the limitations of the foreign-substance and stem-on-stem disqualification rules.

Occasionally a Mini-Flora specimen will possess a stem having only three leaflets. This does not merit concern if the bloom specimen is properly framed and balanced and the exhibit maintains an aesthetic appeal. However if more entries of the same variety are present and all other elements are equal, the specimen possessing a five-leaflet leaf should receive preference.

BALANCE AND PROPORTION

It is most important that the length of the stem be proportional and in balance with the size of the bloom, a characteristic that resides in the eye of the judge. There are no mathematical guidelines for stem length versus bloom size. However, a stem too long or too short to present a pleasing specimen is out of balance and proportion and is subject to penalization. A stem too thick or too thin (spindly) can be a distraction to the total appearance of the specimen and is subject to penalization.

SIZE

The size of the bloom is judged in the same manner as the hybrid tea specimen. All other prime elements being equal the larger bloom of the same variety should be rewarded. Remember—just as with the hybrid tea class there is great variation in bloom size between different varieties. An unusually large specimen of a typically smaller growing variety should take precedence over a smaller bloom of a larger growing variety. Bloom Size and Balance and Proportion must be considered a part of the total evaluation—the one invariably affects the other.

JUDGING SINGLE MINI-FLORAS
Single Mini-Flora blooms are judged by exactly the same standards as those applied to the single hybrid tea.

JUDGING DECORATIVE MINI-FLORAS
Those Mini-Flora varieties that do not present the classical hybrid tea exhibition form, but display a more informal or old garden rose-like form, are often called "decorative" roses. They do not possess the classical high-pointed center but instead may be flat, cupped or with a sunken center. These roses, while not having the qualities that define exhibition form, are nevertheless candidates for all ribbons, including blue. On occasion a variety that is typically decorative may indeed aspire to exhibition form, in which case, it should be rewarded as such and not dismissed simply because the variety usually is decorative. The possibility always exists that a "decorative" Mini-Flora showing exhibition form may occur, and if so this specimen will be eligible for a blue ribbon, depending upon its degree of excellence, and should be considered for a Mini-Flora award.

JUDGING OPEN BLOOM MINI-FLORAS
The open bloom Mini-Floras are judged by exactly the same standards of cleanliness and freshness as those applied to the open bloom hybrid tea specimen.

JUDGING MINI-FLORA SPRAYS
Mini-Flora sprays should be placed in a special class for these roses and be judged by the same standards as floribunda sprays. The individual florets may possess exhibition or decorative form, depending on what is typical of that variety. Judges must know the most perfect phase of beauty for the variety they are judging—for some it is 1/2-3/4 open while others are considered most beautiful at the fully open stage. The spray specimen may be shown with the blooms at the same exhibition stage of opening or in a stages-of-bloom type pattern, depending upon the variety. Judges must remember what is the typical standard for the variety they are judging in regards to form and pattern of opening and penalize if the specimen deviates from this standard. The award for best Mini-Flora spray should go to the specimen exhibiting outstanding attributes of that variety. The foliage should be clean

and free of disease or insect damage. Size is applied to the individual florets and the overall spray. The entire spray is taken into consideration with regards to balance and proportion.

In no case should one bloom flanked by one or more immature (green) buds be considered a spray, and such a specimen should be eliminated from consideration for any award as it does not meet the criteria of a spray. A spray is defined as two or more blooms on a stem.

MINI-FLORA AWARDS

The Mini-Flora Queen, King and Princess of the Show are selected from the one-bloom-per-stem Mini-Flora classes. The best three roses in these classes are eligible for the ARS Gold, Silver and Bronze Mini-Flora Medal Certificate Awards for Mini-Flora Queen, King and Princess of the Show, respectively. The number and titles of any additional specimens to make up a Mini-Flora Court of Honor are at the discretion of the local show committee.

In addition to the Medal Certificates for the one-bloom-per-stem specimens, the ARS offers the following certificates to the best of the blue-ribbon winners in each of the following categories:

Mini-Flora Rose Bowl
Mini-Flora Spray

Appendix C

Mini-Flora Official List

Current as of June 16, 2006

'Absolute Hit'	MinFl, or, dbl.
'Adversity'	MinFl, w, 2005, full
'Affection'	MinFl, mr, semi-dbl.
'Aladdin Palace'	MinFl, ab, 0, dbl.
'Alexa' (MOEalexa)	MinFl, dp, 2001, dbl.
'Alicante'	MinFl, dp, dbl.
'Aliena' (TUCkaliena)	MinFl, yb, 2002, dbl.
'Alto Parade'	MinFl, ab, dbl.
'Amazing Palace'	MinFl, ab, 0, dbl.
'Amber Flash' (WILdak)	MinFl, ob, 1982
'Amber Hit'	MinFl, ab, dbl.
'Amor Hit'	MinFl, dr, 0, dbl.
'Amy Grant' (TUCkamy)	MinFl, lp, 1998, dbl.
'Andie MacDowell'	MinFl, or, 2003, dbl.
'Andrea Parade'	MinFl, m, dbl.
'Andromeda Hit'	MinFl, w, dbl.
'Anneli' (Seaanne)	MinFl, ob, 2004, semi-dbl
'Annette'	MinFl, mp, dbl.
'Ashton' (Welton)	MinFl, pb, 2005, dbl.
'Autumn Bliss' (Welbliss)	MinFl, yb, 2005, full
'Autumn Splendor' (MICautumn)	MinFl, yb, 1999
'Babyface' (Rawril)	MinFl, w, 2000
'Bella Via' (ZIPvia)	MinFl, w, 1991, dbl.
'Belle Hit'	MinFl, lp, dbl.
'Bellissima' (ZIPbell)	MinFl, or, 1988, dbl.
'Betty's Baby' (JUDbaby)	MinFl, dp, 1994, semi-dbl.
'Bijou'	MinFl, pb, 1991
'Blanca Parade'	MinFl, w, dbl.
'Bonbon Hit'	MinFl, yb, semi-dbl.
'Bordeaux Palace'	MinFl, mr, 0, dbl.
'Bowie Yellow Patio'	MinFl, my, 1995
'Brian'	MinFl, mr, dbl.
'Bronze Baby'	MinFl, yb
'Bubikopf'	MinFl, pb, 1986
'Bunter Kobold'	MinFl, yb, 1995

'Butter Cream' (MARbutter)	MinFl, my, 2003, full
'Cachet' (TUCkach)	MinFl, w, 1997
'California Heart' (TINheart)	MinFl, or, 2004, dbl.
'Calypso Hit'	MinFl, dr, dbl.
'Camden' (Houcam)	MinFl, mr, 2002, dbl.
'Camilla Parade'	MinFl, w, dbl.
'Canoodling' (Seaoodle)	MinFl, ob, 2004, semi-dbl
'Capitoule Palace'	MinFl, dr, 0, dbl.
'Cardinal'	MinFl, dr, dbl.
'Caroline Brian'	MinFl, ob, 1997
'Carolyn's Passion' (WILcapa)	MinFl, my, 2006, dbl.
'Charismatic' (DECmatic)	MinFl, rb, 2003, dbl.
'Charmed' (Bricharm)	MinFl, ab, 2001, dbl.
'Checkmate' (Tuckmate)	MinFl, rb, 2002, full
'Chic Parade'	MinFl, lp, dbl.
'Chinese Puzzle' (GELpuzzle)	MinFl, rb, 1999, dbl.
'Chris Jolly'	MinFl, or, 1985, dbl.
'City Lights'	MinFl, dy, 1992
'Clara Parade'	MinFl, w, dbl.
'Class of '73' (TUC30reunion)	MinFl, pb, 2003, dbl.
'Claudia Parade'	MinFl, lp, dbl.
'Colour Magic'	MinFl, pb, 1999
'Colour Parade'	MinFl, or, semi-dbl.
'Columbine Parade'	MinFl, lp, dbl.
'Comedy' (Gelco)	MinFl, yb, 2000, full
'Conundrum' (Tuckpuzzle)	MinFl, yb, 2002, dbl.
'Coral Carpet'	MinFl, mp
'Coral Pagode'	MinFl, pb, dbl.
'Coral Pastel'	MinFl, op
'Corallina'	MinFl, ob, 1993
'Cornelia Hit'	MinFl, my, dbl.
'Corsage'	MinFl, w, semi-dbl.
'Cougar' (Moecougar)	MinFl, rb, 2000, full
'Cream Puff'	MinFl, pb, 1981, semi-dbl.
'Dandenong'	MinFl, or
'Dazzler'	MinFl, op, 1995
'Delight'	MinFl, ab
'Denise Parade'	MinFl, w, semi-dbl.
'Different Charm' (Seacharm)	MinFl, or, 2004, very full.
'Dilly Dilly' (TINdilly)	MinFl, m, 1985, dbl.

'Dolly Dot'	MinFl, dy
'Dolores Marie' (TUCkmarie)	MinFl, m, 2001, very full
'Donnaway Hit'	MinFl, ab, dbl.
'Double Gold' (SAVadouble)	MinFl, yb, 2002, full
'Dr John Dickman' (BRIman)	MinFl, m, 2002, dbl.
'Dr. Troy Garret' (Weltroy)	MinFl, mr, 2005, full
'Dream Lover'	MinFl, mp
'Dyllan's Mom' (Brymom)	MinFl, rb, 2001, dbl.
'Eloise'	MinFl, mp, 2003, dbl.
'Emerald Hit'	MinFl, w, dbl.
'Emily Louise'	MinFl, dy, 0, single
'Equinox' (TUCknox)	MinFl, ob, 2005, full
'Essie Lee' (JUDlee)	MinFl, ob, 1992, dbl.
'Estepona Hit'	inFl, ob, dbl.
'Esther Jasik' (ZIPest)	MinFl, w, 1997, very dbl.
'Fair'	MinFl, mp, dbl.
'Fancy Dancer' (BRIdancer)	MinFl, w, 2002, dbl.
'Fancy Hit'	MinFl, or, dbl.
'Fantasy Hit'	MinFl, dr, semi-dbl.
'Favourite Hit'	MinFl, ab, semi-dbl.
'Ferrin' (Tuckferrin)	MinFl, mp, 2000, dbl.
'Festival'	MinFl, rb, 0
'Fiery Hit'	MinFl, ob, semi-dbl.
'Fireworks'	MinFl, rb, 0, dbl.
'Fitzhugh's Diamond' (Welhugh's)	MinFl, yb, 2005, full
'Flaming'	MinFl, ob, dbl.
'Flamingo'	MinFl, mp, dbl.
'Flirting Palace'	MinFl, mr, dbl.
'Florita'	MinFl, dp, 1994
'Flower Power'	MinFl, ob, 0, dbl.
'Fontana' (Brifont)	MinFl, ab, 2001, dbl.
'Foolish Pleasure' (DECsure)	MinFl, pb, 2003, full
'Fragrant Moon'	MinFl, my, 0, semi-dbl.
'Frilly Dilly'	MinFl, lp, 0
'Fuchsia Sunblaze'	MinFl, op, 0
'Gaia'	MinFl, pb, 1993
'Gail' (TINgail)	MinFl, yb, 1986, dbl.
'Gelber Kobold'	MinFl, dy, 1996
'Gentle Clown'	MinFl, pb, 1994
'Gentleman's Agreement' (BRIgentle)	MinFl, mr, 1998, very dbl.

'Georgia Belle' (Talgeorgia)	MinFl, op, 2000, very full
'Glamour Girl'	MinFl, rb, 1992, single
'Gloria Palace'	MinFl, lp, dbl.
'Gold Country' (Seagold)	MinFl, my, 1987, dbl.
'Gold Patio'	MinFl, dy, 1997
'Golden Anniversary'	MinFl, my, 1997
'Golden Fox'	MinFl, dy, 1997
'Golden Hands'	MinFl, my, 1995
'Golden Hit'	MinFl, dy, semi-dbl.
'Golden Jewel'	MinFl, dy, 1959, dbl.
'Golden Trust'	MinFl, yb, dbl.
'Graceland'	MinFl, op, 1989
'Graduation Day' (Jalgrad)	MinFl, ab, 2004, very dbl.
'Granny's Favourite'	MinFl, op, 0
'Hampton'	MinFl, w, 1996, dbl.
'Hand in Hand'	MinFl, or, 0, double
'Happy Birthday'	MinFl, w, 0
'Happy Times'	MinFl, mp, 0
'Harm Saville' (WEKclauni)	MinFl, dr, 2004, dbl.
'Heartlight' (KINheart)	MinFl, ob, 1985
'Heavens Above' (Webspark)	MinFl, rb, 2003, full
'Hedgefire'	MinFl, mr, 0
'Heidi Parade'	MinFl, mp, 0, dbl.
'Honeybee' (ZLEhoney)	MinFl, ab, 2003, very full
'Hot Parade'	MinFl, dp, dbl.
'House Beautiful'	MinFl, my, 0, double
'Humanity'	MinFl, dr, 0, double
'Indian Silk' (LENlilo)	MinFl, ab, 2000, full
'Ingrid' (MANing)	MinFl, rb, 2005, full
'Isabel Hit'	MinFl, dr, dbl.
'Isolde' (JUDsolde)	MinFl, pb, 1994, dbl.
'Isolde Hit'	MinFl, rb, dbl.
'Ivory Quill'	MinFl, w, 0, double
'Jeanne d'Arc Parade'	MinFl, w, dbl.
'Jennifer Hit'	MinFl, dr, 0, dbl.
'Jerry Lynn' (TUCkjerry)	MinFl, ab, 2004, full
'Jolanda Hit'	MinFl, w, dbl.
'Jolly Good' (LENeli)	MinFl, op, 2000, dbl.
'Jone Asher'	MinFl, 1987
'Joyce'	MinFl, lp, single

'Julie Parade'	MinFl, lp, dbl.
'Kaylee Rose'	MinFl, lp, 2001, very full
'Kim Peters' (Worangry)	MinFl, mp, 2006, full
'Kismet' (TUCkfate')	MinFl, yb, 2005, dbl.
'Lady E'owyn' ('Tuckladye)	MinFl, pb, 2000, full
'Lady Jennifer Green' (Woralps)	MinFl, w, 2006, single
'Lady Parade'	MinFl, mp, 0, dbl.
'Laura' (Gella)	MinFl, rb, 2001, full
'Laurel Louise'	MinFl, ab, 0, double
'Leonie Parade'	MinFl, mr, 0, dbl.
'Liberty Bell' (BENpete)	MinFl, rb, 2003, full
'Liberty Parade'	MinFl, ob, dbl.
'Life Begins at 40' (Horhohoho)	MinFl, w, 2001, dbl.
'Light'	MinFl, my, dbl.
'Limerick' (ZIPlime)	MinFl, rb, 1991, dbl.
'Linda Parade'	MinFl, mp, dbl.
'Little Deb' (WILdeb)	MinFl, or, 2002, semi-dbl
'Little Len'	MinFl, ab, 1987
'Little Ruby'	MinFl, dr, single
'Liza'	MinFl, mr, 1993
'Louisville Lady' (Wellady)	MinFl, dp, 2003, full
'Love Note' (ZIPnote)	MinFl, pb, 1990, full
'Lovebird'	MinFl, mp, 0
'Loyal Friend'	MinFl, w
'Lucky Me' (Socluck)	MinFl, dp, 2003, full
'Luscious Lucy' (TUCklucy)	MinFl, m, 2004, dbl.
'Madeleine'	MinFl, yb, 2005, dbl.
'Madeline Spezzano' (TINmad)	MinFl, mp, 1985
'Madonna'	MinFl, ab, dbl.
'Magic Hit'	MinFl, rb, dbl.
'Mama Mia' (ZIPmia)	MinFl, mp, 1986, dbl.
'Mandarin Silk' (Denman)	MinFl, ob, 2005, full
'Mango Tango' (Geltan)	MinFl, ab, 2000, dbl
'Margaret Denton' (DENmar)	MinFl, rb, 2003, full
'Marianne Hit'	MinFl, my, semi-dbl.
'Marie Christina'	MinFl, lp, 0
'Martina Hit'	MinFl, dr, semi-dbl.
'Martinique Hit'	MinFl, ab, dbl.
'Mary Louise' (BUSmalou)	MinFl, m, 1996, full
'Mary 'n' John' ('Seamary')	MinFl, my, 2000, dbl.

'Mary's Pleasure - The Mary Woods Rose' (Woraugust)

	MinFl, dp, 2006, dbl.
'Maxima Hit'	MinFl, ob, semi-dbl.
'Melody Hit'	MinFl, dp, dbl.
'Memory Hit'	MinFl, ob, dbl.
'Memphis Blues' (Welblue)	MinFl, m, 2005, dbl.
'Memphis Cajun' (Welcajun)	MinFl, m, 2006, full
'Memphis King' (Welking)	MinFl, dr, 2002, full
'Memphis Magic' (Welmagic)	Mini-Flora, dr, 2005, dbl.
'Memphis Music' (Welmusic)	MinFl, rb, 2006, dbl.
'Mette Parade'	MinFl, w, dbl.
'Michelle Claire' (Horseekfell)	MinFl, op, 2001, dbl.
'Mistral Parade'	MinFl, dy, dbl.
'Misty Eyed' (Seamit)	MinFl, w, 2003, dbl.
'Misty Morning' (JUDmorn)	MinFl, m, 1995, dbl.
'Moondance Masquerade' (Jalmoon)	MinFl, w, 2005, full
'Moonlight'	MinFl, ly, dbl.
'Moonlight Scentsation' (SAVamoon)	MinFl, w, 2004, very full.
'Morag Ross' (Horseekship)	MinFl, yb, 2001, dbl.
'Mr J C B'	MinFl, my
'Mrs Mavis Watson' (Woranchor)	MinFl, ly, 2005, dbl.
'Natasja Hit'	MinFl, lp, semi-dbl.
'Nemesis' (TUCknemesis)	MinFl, rb, 2004, dbl.
'New Arrival'	MinFl, or, 1998
'Nicola Parade'	MinFl, pb, dbl.
'Nicole Marie'	MinFl, ly, 2002, full
'Nicoline Parade'	MinFl, or, dbl.
'Night Music' (ZIPmusic)	MinFl, mp, 1988, dbl.
'Noble Hit'	MinFl, mr, dbl.
'Nolpeg'	MinFl, m, 2004, full
'Nolsue'	MinFl, pb, 2004, dbl.
'Northwest Sunset'	MinFl, op
'Orange Seabreeze'	MinFl, op, 1996
'Our Daughter' (Bossufrex)	MinFl, mp, 2001, very full
'Our Son' (Bosrexfolk)	MinFl, mr, 2001, dbl.
'Our Terry' (Webcrimson)	MinFl, dr, 2001, full
'Overnight Scentsation' (SAVanight)	MinFl, mp, 1997, very dbl.
'Patio Dance' (WILpada)	MinFl, rb, 1984, dbl.
'Patio Gold' (WILpago)	MinFl, my, 1984, dbl.
'Patio Jewel'	MinFl, m, 1975, single

'Patio Orange'	MinFl, or
'Patio Patty'	MinFl, yb, 1975, semi-dbl.
'Patio Pearl'	MinFl, pb, 1975, semi-dbl.
'Patio Ribbon'	MinFl, dr, 1975, semi-dbl.
'Patio Snow' (WILpasn)	MinFl, w, 1984, dbl.
'Patriot's Dream' (Micpat)	MinFl, rb, 2000, full
'Peach Delight' (Savapeach)	MinFl, ab, 2001, very full
'Peach Parade'	MinFl, ab, dbl.
'Peach Pastel'	MinFl, ab
'Pearl Anniversary'	MinFl, lp, 1995
'Perfect Hit'	MinFl, dp, dbl.
'Pernille Hit'	MinFl, ob, semi-dbl.
'Peter Cottontail' (Marpeter)	MinFl, w, 2004, dbl.
'Petite Fredaine' (LENlitlit)	MinFl, op, 2000, dbl.
'Pink Patio'	MinFl, lp, 1997
'Pink Pirouette'	MinFl, mp, 1998
'Pippy'	MinFl, pb, 1995
'Polar Cap' (BROcap)	MinFl, w, 2004, dbl.
'Poopsie' (GREfairlynn)	MinFl, w, 2003, full
'Prom Night' (ZIPpro)	MinFl, pb, 1987, very dbl.
'Providence' (TUCprov)	MinFl, my, full
'Pure Hit'	MinFl, w, 1993, dbl.
'Pure Magic'	MinFl, ob, 1999
'Purple Dawn' (BRIdawn)	MinFl, m, 1991, dbl.
'Purple'n'Gold' (MANpurgold)	MinFl, m, 2004, full
'Pzazz Hit'	MinFl, rb, 1996, dbl.
'Quiet Time' (TINquiet)	MinFl, m, 1995, dbl.
'Rachel' (Ricrachel)	MinFl, dp, 2005, full
'Ramona Hit'	MinFl, dp, dbl.
'Raspberry Ice' (ZIPberry)	MinFl, rb, 1988, dbl.
'Ray Still' (HOUstill)	MinFl, mr, 2001, dbl.
'Reah Nicole' (Jalnicole)	MinFl, pb, 2004, full
'Real Hit'	MinFl, dr, dbl.
'Red Pagode'	MinFl, mr, dbl.
'Regina Palace'	MinFl, mp, semi-dbl.
'Renegade'	MinFl, lp, 1995
'Rest in Peace'	MinFl, mp
'Rhona Catherine'	MinFl, dr, 2001, dbl.
'Rialto Palace'	MinFl, w, semi-dbl.
'Rickie-Tickie' (GRErickie)	MinFl, or, 2003, single

'Rio Rita' (Worattack)	MinFl, dy, 2005, dbl.
'Rita Applegate' (TINrita)	MinFl, ly, 1996, very dbl.
'Robin Alonso' (ALOrobin)	MinFl, dr, 2005, full
'Robin Red Breast' (INTerrob)	MinFl, rb, 1983, single
'Roche Centenary'	MinFl, mr, 1993
'Rocky Top' (WELtop)	MinFl, or, 2004, dbl.
'Ronda Palace'	MinFl, mr, semi-dbl.
'Rose Country' (Sprose)	MinFl, lp, 2001, dbl.
'Rose MacKenzie' (Jalmac)	MinFl, dr, 2005, full
'Rosita Parade'	MinFl, yb, semi-dbl.
'Rosy Ann' (LENlitpap)	MinFl, op, 2000, full
'Rosy Pagode'	MinFl, mp, dbl.
'Roxie' (TUCkgrinnel)	MinFl, op, 2001, dbl.
'Royal Flush'	MinFl, pb, 1992
'Royal Palace'	MinFl, yb, dbl.
'Ruffian' (Decruf)	MinFl, op, 2000, dbl.
'Salmon Dream'	MinFl, op, 1999
'San Francisco Sunset' (Seaset)	MinFl, or, 2004, dbl.
'Sarah Anne'	MinFl, mp, 2002, full
'Sassy Cindy' (Bricindy)	MinFl, rb, 2005, full
'Scarlet Hit'	MinFl, mr, 1991, semi-dbl.
'Scarlet Patio'	MinFl, mr, 1993
'Scentillating Blues' (Socblue)	MinFl, m, 2003, dbl.
'Scott Chait' (ZIPcha)	MinFl, ob, 2003, full
'Seattle Sunrise' (MOEseattle)	MinFl, ab, 2005, dbl.
'Sherry Parks Sunrise' (Jalpark)	MinFl, ab, 2005, very full.
'Shrimp Hit'	MinFl, or, semi-dbl.
'Simply Beautiful' (WELodd)	MinFl, m, 2003, dbl.
'Snow Hit'	MinFl, w, dbl.
'Snow Ruby'	MinFl, rb, 1996
'Solar Flair' (Benbaas)	MinFl, yb, 2004, full
'Something for Judy' (TINjudy)	MinFl, pb, 1995, dbl.
'Sonja Parade'	MinFl, yb, dbl.
'Soraya Hit'	MinFl, mp, dbl.
'Spectacular Palace'	MinFl, ab, 0, dbl.
'Spring Palace'	MinFl, pb, 0, dbl.
'Spring's A Comin'' (Welcom)	MinFl, pb, 2001, dbl.
'Stardance' (WILblank)	MinFl, w, 1982, dbl.
'Starlet'	MinFl, w, dbl.
'Starlight Parade'	MinFl, w

'Starship' (BRIstar)	MinFl, yb, 2002, full
'Sterling Parade'	MinFl, mr, 0, dbl.
'Strawberry Fayre'	MinFl, rb
'Sullivan Hit'	MinFl, my, dbl.
'Summer Splash' (PIXsummer)	MinFl, my, 2003, dbl.
'Sun Hit'	MinFl, my, dbl.
'Sun Kissed' (Pixkiss)	MinFl, yb, 2003, full
'Suncharm'	MinFl, dy
'Sundance Palace'	MinFl, dy
'Sunglow Palace'	MinFl, my, dbl.
'Sweet Allison'	MinFl, rb, 1985, dbl.
'Sweet Arlene' (Tinarlene)	MinFl, m, 2001, full
'Sweet Cheeks' (STRjillian)	MinFl, yb, 2003, semi-dbl
'Sweet Dreams'	MinFl, lp
'Sweet Memories'	MinFl, my
'Sweet Tangela' (GELtan)	MinFl, yb, 2002, full
'Sweet Wonder'	MinFl, ab
'Tantalizing Mary' (Seatanta)	MinFl, yb, 2000, full
'Tennessee Sunrise' (Weltenn)	MinFl, ob, 2001, full
'Tennessee Sunset' (Welsun)	MinFl, yb, 2002, full
'Thank You'	MinFl, dp
'Thanks To Sue' (MORsalvatore)	MinFl, ab, 2004, semi-dbl
'The Creakes Rose' (Woramble)	MinFl, ab, 2006, dbl.
'The Governator' (GREnewgov)	MinFl, or, 2003, full
'The Merrion Rose' (KENsheco)	MinFl, rb, 2003, single
'Thelma's Glory' (Jalglory)	MinFl, dp, 2004, semi-dbl
'Tidewater' (BRItide)	MinFl, w, 1991, dbl.
'Tiffany Lite' (GELlite)	MinFl, w, 1998, dbl.
'Tiffany Lynn'	MinFl, pb, 1985
'Tye-Dye' (Seadead)	MinFl, rb, 2006, full
'Vera Roberta Carver' (Worarch)	MinFl, mp, 2005, dbl.
'Violet Hit'	MinFl, m
'Violet Mist'(TINviolet)	MinFl, m, 1993, dbl.
'Virginia Dare'	MinFl, w
'Water Lily' (Jalwater)	MinFl, w, 2004, dbl.
'Whirlaway' (Decwhirl)	MinFl, w, 2005, full
'White Pagode'	MinFl, w, dbl.
'White Quill'	MinFl, w
'Will-o'-the-Wisp'	MinFl, pb
'Wonderful' (Welfull)	MinFl, pb, 2003, full

'Yantai' (TINtai)   MinFl, yb, 1989, dbl.
'Yellow Bird' (WELbyrd)   MinFl, my, 2004, full
'Yellow Pagode'   MinFl, my
'Yellow Paillette'   MinFl, my
'Yellow Quill'   MinFl, my
'Zest For Life' (Worantler)   MinFl, ob, 2005, dbl.

Index

Rose Photos

Photo Credits